Appreciati
Church

A practical Appreciative Inquiry resource for church communities

All shall be well, and all shall be well... For there is a force of love moving through the universe that holds us fast and will never let you go

**Dame Julian of Norwich (c.1342–1416):
first woman to write a book in the English language**

Appreciative Inquiry is a process for engaging people in building the kinds of organisations and a world they want to live in. Working from peoples' strengths and positive experiences, AI co-creates a future based on collaboration and open dialogue.

**David Cooperrider:
founder of Appreciative Inquiry**

Finally, beloved, whatever is true, whatever is honourable, whatever is just, whatever is pure, whatever is pleasing, whatever is commendable, if there is excellence and if there is anything worthy of praise, think about these things.

Philippians 4.8

Appreciating Church – A practical Appreciative Inquiry resource for church communities

Written and edited by Tim Slack, Appreciating People and Fiona Thomas, United Reformed Church
Illustrations by Elizabeth Gray-King
Design by Ken Ashcroft
Proofreading by Lucy Chesters
Publisher: Fiona Shaw
Printed and bound in the UK by Printfine

ISBN 978-0-9955594-1-7

First published in February 2017 by:
Wordscapes Ltd.
The Mezzanine,
Northern Lights Building, Cains Brewery
Grafton Street
Liverpool L8 5SD
www.wordscape.org.uk

www.appreciating.church

Contents

Welcome and introduction

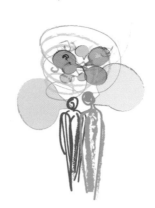

Welcome to *Appreciating Church*, a practical and user-friendly guide to Appreciative Inquiry within churches, organisations and communities. *Appreciating Church* is an ecumenical project initiated and led by the United Reformed Church, in partnership with the Methodist Church, Quakers, and the Congregational Federation, with interest from individual dioceses of the Church of England and others. This resource is part of a programme to create a self-sustaining AI community of practice across the Church. The programme aims to foster and encourage the church at a local and national level to engage people in an inclusive way, listening to 'all the voices', building on our existing strengths and skills, counting our blessings and co-creating a resilient church as part of the Kingdom of Heaven. More information about the *Appreciating Church* story can be found on page 120.

Appreciating Church includes worship materials and information on how to get involved in the AI community of practice. It shares practical understanding of AI theory and practice, experiences of AI within the Church, and useful resources.

As a team, we're thankful to everyone who has contributed content and examples of AI practice.

Appreciating People are UK experts in the use of AI and have been the professional advisers and trainers to the programme, providing core training materials from their range of resources, and giving permission to use content from *AI essentials – a practical guide to Appreciative Inquiry.*

Appreciating Church is supported by the website, www.appreciating.church, which contains information on the AI training programmes, their availability, key local contacts, further AI stories and case studies and additional worship materials. As your AI exploration unfolds, you can share and contribute learning and experience to the community of AI practice on the website.

We hope you enjoy your AI journey as you seek to encourage God's people to flourish.

Fiona Thomas, United Reformed Church
Tim Slack, Appreciating People

Foreword

I am the granddaughter of a Methodist Minister. I am the niece of two uncles and an aunt who are Methodist Ministers, and I am a cousin of a Methodist Minister. To say that I grew up 'appreciating church' is perhaps an understatement. As such, some of my earliest memories involve being with members of my own church community as we came together to support someone in need, or to pool our gifts and talents together to help strengthen our community in both big and small ways. At its heart, I believe that the 21st century Church – regardless of denomination – is all about discovering and lifting up what is best in individuals, communities, and our society as a whole. It is about helping us come together across the political, social, and economic spheres that too often divide us, while inviting us to lift our aspirations and align our actions for the collective good.

At its heart, Appreciative Inquiry (AI) is fundamentally about these same things.

AI, as both an organisational change philosophy and methodology, is all about the search for the best in people, their organisations, and the strength-filled, opportunity-rich world around us. AI invites us to focus our attention on 'what gives life' to our human and ecological systems when they are most generative and vibrant. AI involves asking questions that strengthen a community or organisation's ability to understand, anticipate and heighten its positive potential. It mobilises inquiry through the crafting of 'unconditional positive questions' and can be applied at all levels within a system – from individuals and small teams, to hundreds and sometimes thousands of people. As David Cooperrider, a founding thought leader of AI, once stated: 'appreciative inquiry is a whole set of philosophy and tools that help with the elevation, the magnification and then ultimately the refraction of our highest human strengths out to society.'

Given the kindred spirits that echo within both AI and the Church, I cannot think of a more philosophically aligned methodology for the work of our modern-day churches than AI.

Today, I am still the granddaughter, niece and cousin of ministers, and I continue on my own spiritual journey daily with my children, who constantly invite and inspire me to see the best in the increasingly erratic world around us. I am also fortunate to be the Director for the David L. Cooperrider Center for Appreciative Inquiry in the Stiller School of Business at Champlain College, Burlington Vermont (USA). We are the global Center of Excellence for Appreciative Inquiry and strength-based organisational management. The Center aims to become the global hub for cutting-edge work in Appreciative Inquiry across all organisational sectors. And it is work exactly like this that we are excited to support, celebrate and share.

Tim Slack, and Fiona Thomas – with Church AI practitioners – have created a tremendous resource with *Appreciating Church: A practical Appreciative Inquiry resource for church communities.* From their accessible overview of AI, including the principles that underlie any appreciative approach, to their excellent examples of what this work looks like in the context of the church, they have crafted a tool kit that will be useful for anyone in the church, from lay members to leaders.

Appreciative Inquiry reminds us that we live in a world that our questions create. Thus, I invite you to be inquisitive and use your imagination when you open this guidebook. Ask yourself, what is the world calling you to do? What is the true, the good, the better and the possible that is stirring in your soul that you want to tap into? How can you be a light in the darkness and invite others to shine their light as well?

I look forward to seeing how our world positively shifts as you seek answers to these generative questions!

Lindsey Godwin, Ph.D.
Professor of Management, Stiller School of Business
Director, Cooperrider Center for Appreciative Inquiry
Champlain College
Burlington, Vermont, USA
appreciativeinquiry@champlain.edu
http://www.champlain.edu/appreciativeinquiry

Why is Appreciative Inquiry important to the Church?

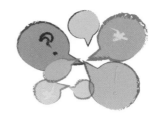

A few years ago a Liverpool church decided to use Appreciative Inquiry to consider its future. In the myriad conversations that took place, a project title emerged – 'count your blessings'. The term comes from a 19th century hymn by Methodist Minister, Johnson Oatman. Two lines in the refrain are:

'Count your blessings name them one by one
Count your blessings see what the Lord hath done'

These words help to explain why Appreciative Inquiry is important to the 21ˢᵗ century Church. The words of Julian of Norwich at the beginning of the book add to this view. As part of the co-creation process, the ecumenical partners were asked to give their views about why AI is important in church life. Their responses are striking in their similar views and simplicity – a number of common themes emerged, indicating the ways that AI can help congregational life flourish:

- Reminding us of what people do well in their churches and faith communities, no matter how small the congregation;

- Discovering what works in the Church – the small and large things;

- Recognising the importance of peoples' skills and experiences, and finding ways of building on them;

- Reminding us that we all make a difference – no matter how small;

- Becoming aware of the latent creativity within the people of the church to move things forward. AI offers enjoyable ways to clarify a common purpose and bring about fuller engagement;

- Recognition of the importance of story, dialogue and hearing all the voices from an inclusive standpoint.

AI encourages us to move from the view of a church in decline – with problems to be solved – to a view of creative possibility which energises people, encourages them to do different things, and to be more resilient in adversity.

As the Venerable Guy Elsmore, the Archdeacon of Buckingham, says:

'AI is rooted in an abundant theology of blessing, rather than in the shortcomings which we are often all too well aware of. For the Church, Appreciative Inquiry can provide ways into the future which grow organically from the seeds of the spirit, sometimes hidden or dormant from within Church life.'

Appreciative Inquiry has its roots in organisational development (OD), so has a link to management theory and practice, which parts of the Church have tried to include and adapt in recent years. Such ideas can, however, bring with them a language of goals, targets, and 'management speak', which may not fit with the aims and motivations of many people in churches.

AI is very different from more conventional OD practices. This is exemplified by SOAR™ (Strengths, Opportunities, Aspirations and Results/Resources) which is the AI equivalent of a the familiar SWOT analysis (Strengths, Weaknesses, Opportunities, and Threats). Later in this book you will see a spiritual journey exercise based around SOAR™ which has been used individually and collectively with interest and enthusiasm. It would be hard to imagine a SWOT version being engaging, fruitful or motivating. As someone said on a recent AI training course: 'would you rather help the Church 'soar' or help 'swot' it'?

Since *Appreciating Church* began in early 2014, the ecumenical partnership has grown organically into a major initiative. By the end of April 2017 there will be over 250 people trained across the Church, and a myriad of AI church projects are being delivered.

> **Importance and value of the Appreciative Inquiry to the Church**
>
> *'"We want an inquiry" usually means "let's find out what's gone wrong and who's to blame!" But what we need in every situation is to reflect with the wonder of a child, the maturity to be ever open to listen and learn, and the courage to let new ideas and stories that emerge, shape our future together. "We want Appreciative Inquiry", means a commitment to a way that encourages and enables everyone in the Church to be involved; to know their story is heard and matters; and to see their strengths and achievements valued, as they become recognised as building blocks to move us to how we need to be. The more I see of AI in action, the more I see the way of Christ in his engagement with people. This is why Yorkshire Synod has covenanted to explore this journey together.'*
>
> Revd Kevin Watson, moderator of the General Assembly United Reformed Church, 2016-2018 and URC Moderator Yorkshire Synod

> *'We're a funny lot, human beings, and Christian human beings can be even odder. We know we flourish when we are appreciated, but we tend to grumble and blame and talk each other down instead. When we want change, it is because we think things are wrong, and say so. And here I am doing the same thing! Appreciative Inquiry starts from a different place; from the stories people tell, from the value that already exists; and from the potential for transformation. The process works by hearing and engaging everyone through structured conversations, and it has the potential to lead to positive change, which is embraced by everyone who has participated.'*
>
> Revd Dr Janet Wootton, Director of Learning and Development, Congregational Federation

AI in context

AI is also building an illustrious international history – in 1999 David Cooperrider was invited to design a series of dialogues among 25 of the world's top religious leaders, started by His Holiness the Dalai Lama, who said: 'If only the world's religious leaders could just know each other, the world will be a better place.' Using AI, the group held meetings in Jerusalem and at the Carter Center with President Jimmy Carter.

'It strikes me that we are wedded to a narrative of decline and a conversation that sees the church as a problem rather than as a place of creativity and huge possibility – wellsprings of the Spirit if you like. Appreciative Inquiry seems to me a natural model for churches which want to break out of the "problem cycle" and release energy in re-imagining the future. Strength based approaches are tried and tested across a number of organisations and help to structure conversation in a way which builds upon where energy is already found, directing it in a way that identifies realistic and achievable outcomes. That's why I think that AI has a lot to offer the church in making sense of its opportunities for mission and ministry.'

Revd Richard Andrew, Director of Learning and Development, The Methodist Church

AI has been around for over 30 years and has been used all over the world, from Nepali villages to the UN. Some of the early AI developers were people of the Church who drew on liberation theology, the work of Paulo Freire, and their own church lives.

At a Methodist Church AI training course in October 2016, participants explored the explanation of the AI principles taken from this book (page 21). They felt that *Appreciating Church* may be unique in the lexicon of organisational development resources, in the way it has tried to integrate biblical insights and direct church experience with organisational development practices.

Paul Chaffee writes: 'AI offers a perspective that seeks out the goodness in any system of relationships and then gives participants ways to magnify and give life to that goodness. The initial jolt I experienced upon encountering AI came in the form of a stunning realisation that it systematically delivered on values the Christian family holds high but often fails to embody, such as taking 'the least of these my children' as seriously as everyone else in the community, and booting the debilitating judgmentalism that so often polarises and shreds faith families.[1]

'Appreciative questions call for answers that reveal appreciation, achievement, success, and important experiences, big or small, rather than breakdown and failure. They seek the commendable and steer away from judgment. They attend to memories, feelings, and imagination as well as analysis and opinions. Appreciative interviews allow people to safely pour out their hearts about what is good in their lives, and the result is new, often unexpected relationships and a shared energy that discourages quarrels and undercuts fears of inadequacy.

'Because people have so much difficulty at first talking about success and achievement without a counterpoint of problems and breakdowns, practitioners learn to listen with enormous patience and to keep reframing the situation, always moving away from "understanding the problem" and toward "co-creating a transformed future... Participants quit treating issues like wrestling matches and begin collaborating on what really matters."'

In some ways the title *Appreciating Church* sums it up – how can we all benefit from appreciating how being part of a church or Quaker meeting feeds our spiritual life and supports God's work?

1 www.congregationalresources.org – *A guide to congregational resources for building congregational vitality*, chapter 4. Richard Bass, Editor (Alban Institute, 2005)

Guidance on how to use *Appreciating Church*

The content is organised so that it can be dipped into for advice and guidance on specific ideas, or read consecutively to gain an overview. There are helpful hints along the way on how to use the content effectively.

- Explanations of AI theory and practice includes practical and biblical examples to help understanding and context

- Practical examples and advice permeate the text

- Examples of tools, where appropriate, are downloadable from the *Appreciating Church* website

- Worship materials are included for use when exploring AI projects in Church settings

- Stories are included to illustrate the AI principles and tools from practice

- Information on page 120 explains how the user of this resource can become part of the *Appreciating Church* community of practice

- The images placed throughout the text highlight when the AI principles and tools are at play, helping to reinforce the learning.

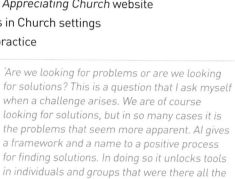

'Are we looking for problems or are we looking for solutions? This is a question that I ask myself when a challenge arises. We are of course looking for solutions, but in so many cases it is the problems that seem more apparent. AI gives a framework and a name to a positive process for finding solutions. In doing so it unlocks tools in individuals and groups that were there all the time and just needed a different approach. When working with AI in Quaker communities I recall occasions when I have heard people say "I have been doing this for years and now I have a name for what I have been doing".'

Oliver Waterhouse, Quaker Life Network Development Officer, Religious Society of Friends

Introduction
to Appreciative
Inquiry

1

PART ONE:
Introduction to Appreciative Inquiry

Much of the AI content included in *Appreciating Church* has been drawn from Appreciating People's resources, in particular *AI essentials*, with extracts from *Taste of AI* and *Creating Great Conversations*. The biblical and spiritual content has been developed by the ecumenical partners. There are many different possible biblical and spiritual interpretations, and we encourage people to foster their understanding of the AI principles and tools by adding their own interpretations and stories. The more you start to look at the bible through an AI lens, the more that texts emerge which relate to the AI principles.

First developed by David Cooperrider in the late 1980s at Case Western University, USA, and now used all over the world, AI is a collaborative and highly participative, system-wide approach to organisation and community development. It identifies and enhances the 'life-giving forces' that are present when a team, organisation, or business is working at its best, serving whatever is its purpose and role. A major influence in the development of Appreciative Inquiry was the work and writings of Jane Magruder Watkins, who first encouraged and led its practical application, and who also trained Appreciating People. Much of this early work took place through international development work. There's more about the history of AI on the *Appreciating Church* website – www.appreciating.church.

The term 'appreciative' comes from the idea that when something increases in value, it 'appreciates'. AI focuses on the generative possibilities – the things that, if increased, would add value and make a difference. 'Inquiry' describes the process of seeking to understand through questions, and the value of paying attention to processes and people.

> The point is this: the one who sows sparingly will also reap sparingly, and the one who sows bountifully will also reap bountifully. Each of you must give as you have made up your mind, not reluctantly or under compulsion, for God loves a cheerful giver. And God is able to provide you with every blessing in abundance, so that by always having enough of everything, you may share abundantly in every good work.
>
> 2 Corinthians 9.8

It is a transformative process focusing on strengths – rather than weaknesses – and encourages active and effective participation. The resulting actions are based on reality, 'owned' by the participants, and much more likely to be deliverable than a prescription devised from outside the situation.

AI is a philosophy, an approach, and a way of working from an appreciative, positive and strength-based standpoint. AI can be used in and adapted to traditional organisational and community development approaches – it's exceptionally flexible, and looks simple in many ways, but is very subtle. It is NOT a set of techniques. Effective practitioners commit themselves to a personal journey to 'be Appreciative Inquiry' in self, in relationships, and in organisations or communities[1]. Appreciative journaling encourages this personal journey and has obvious connections with established spiritual practices such as the Ignatian *Examen*[2] and Wesley's questions for self-examination.

> 'It's been argued that AI's most congruent, comfortable context ultimately will be the faith family because congregations already encourage AI's emphasis on values, storytelling, visioning, and serving the highest good— activities easier for a church council or pastor to broach than a corporation board or its CEO. In fact, Cooperrider's father was a Lutheran pastor who struggled painfully for years before successfully integrating his congregation racially, a drama that did not go unnoticed by a son who subsequently dedicated his life to community transformation without the acid etch of protracted conflict.'
>
> Paul Chaffee 2005

The theology at the heart of *Appreciating Church* is 'about a God of abundance, not pain and fear or scarcity, and how we can use our strengths collectively.' (Robyn Stratton-Berkessel)

AI is used by governments, aid agencies and in the voluntary sector all over the world – from small villages in Nepal and India, to multinational organisations. It has been used by churches in Scotland, Canada and the USA. It can also be used in coaching and in personal development, and AI tools are used within the processes of Asset Based Community Development (ABCD).

---

1   See Nourish to Flourish section in AIP – AI Practitioner Quarterly journal aipractitioner.com/

2   See Part three, example six (page 99)

The unique aspects of AI

AI is different to traditional problem-solving approaches and much of existing organisation development practice – there is a growing understanding that 'if you look for problems, you'll find and create more problems'. It builds on the research showing that people become stronger and build their strengths when working from strengths (see Marcus Buckingham on Strengthsfinder, and VIA character strengths www.viacharacter.org/www/ – you'll find more information in the reading list on page 122).

> 'AI draws mutual appreciation together with the search for next steps. It fosters a way of being Church that moves away from top down hierarchy to a place of shared knowledge and self-organising processes.'
>
> Robin Greenwood Sharing God's Blessing

It's not about positive thinking – although positivity is important. It accepts that there are problems, but looks at them from a different viewpoint and encourages generativity, collaboration, hope and creativity. (You'll find an explanation of generativity on page 19.) AI is also about whole system change – it involves everyone in the room – and AI practitioners often liken its improvised style to playing jazz[3].

The benefits and effectiveness of AI

- It builds relationships enabling people to be known in their relationship, rather than their role
- It creates an opportunity for people to be heard
- It generates opportunities for people to dream and to articulate their dreams
- It creates an environment in which people feel able to choose how they contribute
- It gives people both discretion and the support to act
- It encourages and enables people to be positive

However, In a 'command and control' organisation, or where there is no 'buy in', or understanding at the top of an organisation, then AI is less likely to fulfil its potential. It is, at its heart, about 'create and engage'.

AI and the Church – the Welwyn Garden City testimony

This personal AI testimony provides a practical example of the impact of AI, both personally, and its value in supporting church life.

An interview between Revd Jane Weedon, URC Minister Welwyn Garden City and Tim Slack, Appreciating People

> 'It is important to recognise that AI is not a miracle salve, not a set of self-help exercises or a one-chapter story. Instead, it is an empowering epistemological perspective that personalises, honours, and learns from a community's best accomplishments and most precious values. Then it opens the horizon to take us miles beyond self-interest and old expectations, all the while staying grounded in the commitment bringing us to community in the first place.'
>
> Paul Chaffee 2005

Tim: How did you discover AI and why is it important to you?

Jane: I discovered AI when I was about two years into a new ministry and I couldn't get the church to look to the future at all. Roberta Rominger, the Synod Moderator at the time, suggested that I read Mark Lau Branson's book *Memories, Hopes and Conversations*[4]. I suddenly thought, 'this is brilliant!' because this gives the church permission to look back and see what has been wonderful and has worked well in the past – and that becomes the basis to build on and to dream for the future. It became really important as an amazing approach, to unlock where the church was shut down and couldn't move. I've discovered it can be used in all sorts of contexts.

Tim: When you say 'shut down', what do you mean?

Jane: They couldn't look to the future. All they would do was look to the past, as if they daren't look to the future and were almost afraid there wasn't a future for them somehow.

---

3   Yes to the Mess: Surprising Leadership Lessons from Jazz
4   See reading list page 123

Tim: How has AI affected your ministry?

Jane: It has greatly affected my ministry, because I've learned a lot more about asking those open and appreciative questions. You can use them in a one-to-one conversation, or you can do a whole AI event. The energy flows from people once they start to recall and remember the things that have been good for them. They can see how God has used them in the past and might continue to use them in the future.

Tim: How long have you been using the AI approach?

Jane: I read the book initially in 2009/10, so I've been using it since then.

Tim: And it influenced your work throughout that period?

Jane: Very much so.

Tim: Let's start with the Welwyn Garden City Church story and experience. What was the inquiry? What did you hope to achieve from it? What was your plan?

Jane: The inquiry was into our vision for our future: 'What is God's vision for the future for this church?'

Tim: Using the 'definition' stage, how did you identify your inquiry?

Jane: I hoped to identify some areas that we would work on that would lead us forward from where we were. And I was hoping to discover some quick wins along the way, so we could continue to enthuse people about the process. Once we discovered what the DNA of the church was, we would see how we could work on those areas for the future.

Tim: What were the approach and activities? What did you do?

Jane: The very first thing was to introduce the idea of AI in January 2010. Before then, the Elders had all read the book and had been working on potential questions to ask one another. We had a retreat day in January 2010 and I introduced the idea of AI and it was then that I got the feedback – 'We don't like the term'. They didn't like it being called AI, because it sounded too much like business jargon – that's when I came up with the idea that the conversation process at the beginning would be called *Collecting the Stones*, based on Joshua telling the Elders to collect the stones from the dry river bed after they crossed into the promised land to remind them of God's faithfulness.

Tim: In the Bible, what did Joshua collect the stones for?

Jane: The priests, carrying the Ark of the Covenant, stood in the river Jordan and when they did, the water stopped and the children of Israel passed safely into the Promised Land (Joshua chapters 3&4). When everyone was safely through, the Lord told Joshua to choose 12 men, one from each of the tribes of Israel and to go to the riverbed and pick up a stone, carry it back on their shoulders and build a memorial.

They created a pillar so that everybody could come and show it to their children and tell them the history – how God had been faithful to them in the past and remind them that God would be faithful in the future. It seemed an appropriate story, as we were asking questions about what brought people to this church and when they had felt most alive and engaged in the life of this church. It was looking to the past, so these memories were the stones they were bringing, reminding them of God's faithfulness and that God will be faithful to us in the future.

Tim: What happened next?

Jane: First came the conversations on the second of the Ds (discovery). We worked out what questions we would ask, and all of the Elders tried them out by interviewing each other. We'd trained one or two non-serving Elders, so they came as well and joined in that process and we tried to interview everybody in the congregation. One or two declined but, for the most part, we got most of the congregation who were capable of having a conversation. Even those who were housebound joined in the conversation process.

Tim: And that was over a period of time?

Jane: Yes, over a couple of months. Then we collated all the replies, worked out where all the strands were coinciding in the answers and, quite naively, came up with too many. We had about seven; four or five would be much more sensible. Then we expanded our conversations on each of the subjects by having an 'at home' morning. We used a World Café [5] type space so people could move around the tables and write things on the table cloths and some elders helped host each table to lead people through that.

Tim: Was that a half day event bringing the church together, or part of the service, or a weekend event?

Jane: It was a half day event and we created *Provocative Propositions*[6] from that. Not really knowing 100% what we were doing they were too long, but they were stories of what we hoped for the future. Also, in the middle of it all – as we began the process and I introduced it to people before we had the conversations – we had an exercise asking people if they left Welwyn Garden City Church and came back in five years, what they hoped to find. All of that fed into the collating of the information that we got back.

Tim: You were using the 'dream' phase in the statement – 'If you come back in five years' time'?

Jane: Yes, that was interesting because the dream was specifically focused on what people would want to find in the church. That worked out slightly different from the three wishes that people had for the future.

Tim: Interesting. Why was that?

Jane: When people are asked what three wishes they would have they are very personal – in many of those wishes I found people were looking back to what they had enjoyed in the past. So they would have liked to have seen things revived instead of really looking to the future. That's why I decided, having seen the wishes, that it would be good to ask: 'if we went away and came back in five years, what would we hope to find?'

Tim: I agree with you about the three wishes approach and personally don't use it a lot. I prefer: 'what's the first thing you'll do?' and, 'what's the most radical thing?'.

Jane: That's why we used the dream of what they hoped to find here, saying: 'now you have come back to visit in five year's time and tell us what your experience is'. So it was really dreaming. They had the one experience of dreaming what they wanted to see and then I put them in that place of imagining that they had actually been to a service and as they were leaving, thinking, *'wow. This is wonderful!'* I asked, 'what have you experienced then?' That was actually slightly different. It was interesting.

Tim: After you had the 'at home', what was next?

Jane: We had a special service where everybody had a stone to take away with them for a week to give thanks for all sorts of things. Whenever and whatever they wanted to say thank you to God for, to hold onto that stone at least once a day – it was like a version of your gratitude journal – *Food for Thought* for a week. Then they brought the stone back on Sunday and we created a cairn and placed round it all of the booklets (we created booklets for the conversations to be recorded in). We photographed that and recorded and celebrated what we had done so far.

Tim: After all that process, you continued working with it. What happened next?

Jane: Then we went onto the next stage which was more dreaming I guess. Asking ourselves where we thought we needed to start, and what was the first step we wanted to go on with. I think the next step was remembering the future. It might have been the 'extraordinary future' next, creating an image of what that extraordinary future might look like.

We took those provocative proposals and asked ourselves where to start. We started creating a notice board with all of this on it, so it became a visual image. Underneath each strand was a card that said what the strand was. One was a 'welcoming and friendly church' and underneath it was the provocative proposition. A bit like a family tree – what came off from it were the things we had done to develop in that area. So we ran a course.

---

5   www.theworldcafe.com/ See this example of blending AI and World Café http://positivitystrategist.com/appreciative-inquiry-workshop-and-world-cafe-blend-farms-in-the-city/
6   See Card 17 in http://www.appreciatingpeople.co.uk/ai-essentials-cards/

Tim: It became a plan. An organic plan that grew out of the process?

Jane: Yes. The first thing we did was run *Everybody Welcome,* which is a course for the church to become much more welcoming and open. That was part of that. Being a welcoming church still continues because other things have come into it. The URC has Vision 2020 now and so our focus for this year is 'hospitality and diversity' – one thought that is ongoing is that we might scrap the welcome team and call it a hospitality team. We'll think about it from a very different perspective so you're not just shoving a hymn book in someone's hand when they come in on Sunday morning. What is it to be hospitable when somebody arrives in Church?

Tim: You've taken the original proposition, continually refining and updating it. It evolves.

Jane: Yes it keeps on evolving, we've still got those strands.

Tim: What you have been able to do is integrate the process into the life and work of the church.

Jane: It's become part of the process. When we had a planning day this year, an 'at home', the first thing I did was to fish out all of those dreams from 2010/11 and asked people to look at them and see what we had achieved. They could see what had been accomplished and how far we had actually moved from where we were to where we are now. People were shocked at the amount that had changed. They were really, really shocked.

Tim: Shocked in a nice way?

Jane: Absolutely, yes. They could not believe we had achieved all these things we had dreamed and set out to achieve. They hadn't even noticed – because it had been done. You know if someone had come in and said: 'we are going to do X', and just enforced something on people, then they would have resisted it. But, because it was part of the conversation and it became organic and a natural way of developing things, then it has just happened without that resistance, and it has gained a life of its own really and taken off.

Tim: Reflecting on your experience what have you learned in the process, what have you gained from it?

Jane: It has developed my way of working an awful lot, I guess. I still don't do it 100% naturally; I don't necessarily think about what principle this relates to and that sort of thing. Sometimes when I am stuck I will just sit there and think. Going back to the principles then helps me to find the first step in something that has got a bit blocked up.

Tim: Very true.

Jane: It is becoming much more of a natural process for me. But it is so Gospel, isn't it? Whatever is good, whatever is true, think on these things. But that is so my Gospel anyway.

Tim: That is an absolutely brilliant story

Jane: And what has come out of it is we ended up applying for and getting a grant for a Youth and Children and Families Worker and also for our Mission Co-ordinator. Even if we haven't always got the personnel in the church to support it, we now have employees who are naturally taking it all forward so that has helped as well. That brings its own challenges too, of course.

Tim: Because of the process, have you found that the challenges can be dealt with in a more effective way?

Jane: I am using it as well now in Church Meeting. People sit round tables with good open questions to ask on subjects we need to discuss and we are actually getting through Church Meeting quicker than when we just all sat there looking at each other.

Tim: And is Church Meeting more interesting?

Jane: I think people find it so, yes. Everyone gets to have a say round a table as there are only four or five of you and for the most part you will sit with those you know, so you are not anxious about saying your opinion with them. Then one person feeds back what's been said.

Tim: Thank you for sharing your experience and AI journey.

Appreciative Inquiry: Concepts And Theories

Social Constructionism

Appreciative Inquiry is strongly influenced by the field of Social Constructionism and one of its core principles is based upon the approach. The concept of social constructionism predates AI. In the late 1960s, Peter Berger and Thomas Luckman argued that what we accept as knowledge, what we consider to be true – including the most basic everyday realities of our lives and objects – is derived from our socialisation and social interactions, rather than an inherent quality in any one thing or experience. We then form groups, institutions and spheres of influence that help reinforce and maintain that constructed reality. Ken Gergen is one of the thinkers whose work influenced AI's inclusion of the principle of constructionism.

"There is no such thing as immaculate perception. What you see is what you thought before you looked. Beliefs and theories direct our thoughts, and these thoughts mould our perceptions. These perceptions then direct our actions."

Myron Tribus

Current leading thinkers on constructionism argue that it doesn't belong to any one individual, but has developed as a group of ideas coming together. It's not fixed or frozen – and can itself be seen as a social construct.

We create meaning through social interaction and collectively agreed indicators such as:

- Language – a system of sounds; a series of lines
- Symbols – a national flag; use of metaphor like fire for danger
- Colour – black and white as good and bad; gender-related colours
- Gestures – in many western countries, 'thumbs up' is an endorsement; in Iraq, Iran and Thailand, it's an obscene gesture
- Categories of people – gender, class structure, faith, political, race, sexuality

Social constructions are powerful collectively held beliefs, which rely on three stages of socialisation:

- Primary – the basic rules of society, usually learned from parents
- Secondary – childhood to adolescence, when we learn beliefs from our education, religion, country, institutions and groups
- Reality maintenance – in adulthood maintaining our subjective and socially-constructed world through everyday communication, pursuits and endeavours

"There is no value neutral interpretation of anything," says Gergen.

Key beliefs of a constructionist stance are:

- A critical and questioning approach to what we take for granted as knowledge and truth;
- Our understanding of the world is dependent on where we are in the world, and is historically and culturally specific to our time and place;
- Knowledge and reality are maintained by our social interaction and relationships and are the source of what is true for us;
- Knowledge and social action go together.

Gergen argues for the creation of 'generative theory' which challenges the status quo and develops new repertoires for thought and action. This can be seen as controversial, as it questions concepts of truth, objectivity, value and sense of self.

Examples:

Social movements such as the civil rights movement and feminism are collective efforts to change socially constructed, accepted and endorsed behaviour and ideas. When passionately contested, social constructs can be the catalyst for conflict and for change.

Critics of social constructionism argue that it doesn't take into account how serious influences confine our constructs. They include: power; physicality; materiality (or your wealth and social position).

The application of constructionist ideas has huge potential, because:

- It neither specifies the margins of the discipline, nor fixes the parameters of inquiry in advance
- It is psychologically closely tied to cultural life; inviting passionate engagement
- It links intellectual work with change-oriented practices
- It favours provocative dialogue
- It fires the imagination of futures, yet retains considerable humility toward its own assumptions and respect for the assumptions of others.

(from *Social Psychology as Social Construction: The Emerging Vision* by Kenneth J. Gergen)

Understanding social construction through Church examples

When addressing the theory of social constructionism with churches, there are a number of ways of connecting with elements which may be familiar to church people of varying backgrounds. For example, the existence of different denominations and varying understandings of communion could be included in a discussion of social constructionism. The suggestions given here are offered as possible starting points. As with the rest of this *Appreciating Church* resource, you are encouraged to use your imagination and keep looking for apt illustrations.

When people grasp the idea of social constructionism they realise that their perceptions are prone to shifting. What they believe – and what the person sitting next to them believes – are both shaped by the experiences that have brought them to where they are today. So a way of helping people to see this is to change slightly the way things are done:

- Use contemporary songs in unfamiliar spiritual settings [7] so that the words which are apparently secular take on a new significance. Examples could include Chrissie Hynde's *I'll stand by you* in a reconciliation service, or refer to the Manic Street Preacher's album *This is my truth, tell me yours*, which is taken from a quote by the Labour politician Aneurin (Nye) Bevin.

- Use contemporary translations of the Bible so that people hear familiar passages in fresh ways[8].

- It can also be enlightening to read the Bible with people from different cultures and age-groups. Recent migrants might have a different take on the story of Ruth. Should she have let go of her original identity so easily?

- Sing familiar hymns to unfamiliar tunes.

- Imagine walking a mile in someone else's shoes.

Advice 17 in Quaker faith & practice 1.02
Do you respect that of God in everyone though it may be expressed in unfamiliar ways or be difficult to discern? Each of us has a particular experience of God and each must find the way to be true to it. When words are strange or disturbing to you, try to sense where they come from and what has nourished the lives of others. Listen patiently and seek the truth which other people's opinions may contain for you. Avoid hurtful criticism and provocative language. Do not allow the strength of your convictions to betray you into making statements or allegations that are unfair or untrue. Think it possible that you may be mistaken.

Our deepest fear is not that we are inadequate. Our deepest fear is that we are powerful beyond measure. It is our light not our darkness that most frightens us. We ask ourselves, who am I to be brilliant, gorgeous, talented and fabulous? Actually, who are you not to be? You are a child of God. Your playing small does not serve the world. There's nothing enlightening about shrinking so that other people won't feel insecure around you. We were born to make manifest the glory of God that is within us. It's not just in some of us; it's in everyone. And as we let our own light shine, we unconsciously give other people permission to do the same. As we are liberated from our own fear, our presence automatically liberates others. Marianne Williamson, in A Return to Love (1992), Harper Collins.

---

7   Male female slave or free / Peaceful or disorderly Maybe you and he will not agree / But you need him to show you new ways to see
Bruce Cockburn – *Maybe The Poet*
8   The Aramaic language version may offer additional interpretations....

Biblical insights

Social construction theory says that perceptions and memories are affected by present experience – a biblical example is the way in which the Hebrew slaves forgot how oppressed they were in Egypt: *"The rabble among them had a strong craving; and the Israelites also wept again, and said, 'If only we had meat to eat! We remember the fish we used to eat in Egypt for nothing, the cucumbers, the melons, the leeks, the onions, and the garlic; but now our strength is dried up, and there is nothing at all but this manna to look at.'"* Numbers 11.4-6

Relationships and understanding change together, as is seen in the dynamic between Jesus and his disciples: *"I do not call you servants any longer, because the servant does not know what the master is doing; but I have called you my friends, because I have made known to you everything that I have heard from my father."* John 15.15

The last remaining resources can be the end or the beginning of something, as seen in the story of Elijah and the widow of Zarephath. 1 Kings 17:7-16.

Our perceptions of a situation direct our actions. In the parable of the prodigal son, the younger brother – who claims his inheritance – comes to see what he has lost and is prepared to take drastic action when desperate. Luke 15.11 – 32.

We start from one view of a situation, and arrive at a new view of the situation through conversation with someone who brings a different perspective. This is seen on the road to Emmaus. Luke 24.13-35.

The responsibility which someone feels for a situation can lead them to actions which are not necessary, when others have acted in unexpected ways. The way that Christians see the world – as belonging to God – can be transformative for the people around them, as seen in the story of Paul, Silas and their jailers. Acts 16.23-34

Generativity

Generativity is a key concept in Appreciative Inquiry, especially in the design and delivery phases – you'll see it as a recurring theme in these sections.

"AI can be generative in a number of ways. It is the quest for new ideas, images, theories and models that liberate our collective aspirations, alter the social construction of reality and, in the process, make available decisions and actions that were not available or did not occur to us before. When successful, AI generates spontaneous, unsupervised, individual, group and organisational action toward a better future."

Gervase Bushe

Positivity without generativity can make AI a fleeting experience, rather than transformational and long lasting.

What is it, and why is it important?

Essentially, 'generativity' means generating new (and actionable) ideas – often made possible by the understanding that a different construction of reality is possible. All AI should be generative – it is an idea that underpins all AI practice. Its unique, appreciative style is designed to energise and inspire by challenging assumptions and raising fundamental questions.

So, generativity is crucial to AI – it takes a bit of time to understand, but it's important, and worth the effort. We'll give you some more resources to have a look at later...

Theodore Zeldin says: *"Conversation is a meeting of minds with different memories and habits. When minds meet, they don't just exchange facts: they transform them, reshape them, draw different implications from them, engage in new trains of thought. Conversation doesn't just reshuffle the cards: it creates new cards."*

The concept of generative theory

Kenneth Gergen's concept of generativity is key to understanding AI theory and practice. He describes generative theory as: *'theory that unsettles common assumptions, and opens up possibilities or new forms of action'.*

AI is particularly effective in creating the conditions where generativity can happen. It occurs when individuals and/or a group work from their imagination, creativity, strengths and positive experiences, which creates new working arrangements, fresh ideas, and leads to transformation.

The nature of AI means that it can act as a catalyst, and is particularly good at supporting generativity. Once you've been in a few AI-influenced meetings you'll begin to notice generativity showing up.

"The early image of Appreciative Inquiry was that it would be a form of inquiry that would support generativity – its impact would come from the creation of new ideas, perceptions, metaphors, images and theories that furnished better alternatives for organisational actions."

David Cooperrider and Suresh Srivastva

As we've said, it can take some time to get your head around the idea of generativity, but stick with it – it's extremely inspiring. For further information have a look at www.gervase.bushe.ca.

Helpful hints:

• The appreciative interview is a vital tool in supporting and encouraging generativity;

• As the focus moves from deficit and problem solving, don't be blinkered by focusing exclusively on the positive and ignoring difficult issues. Encourage exploration of the challenges and problems through focusing on what could be done differently;

• It is the interplay of positivity and generativity that supports change and transformation. Gervase Bushe's work (2007) indicates that 'generativity and positivity are both possible without each other, but that positivity by itself does not promote long-lasting change'.

Understanding generativity through church examples

"I came that they may have life, and have it abundantly." John 10.10

When introducing the theory of generativity to churches, it's worth reminding people about the presence and action of the Holy Spirit, which brings newness of life and transforms reality in unexpected ways.

Points to reflect on:

• Churches and congregations may remember times when the decisions they have made have been informed by the movement of the spirit as much as by facts and figures. New ideas emerge when people take time to pray without anxiety.

• Christians are asked to trust in God's grace and generosity, *"The fruit of the Spirit is love, joy, peace, patience, kindness, generosity, faithfulness, gentleness, and self-control. There is no law against such things."* Galatians 5. 22-23

• Relating positively to one another as people, rather than the roles being occupied, can give space for trust to develop and new ways forward to emerge.

• Being a forgiven and forgiving community can create an environment in which generativity flourishes.

• Generativity is often evident in communities that have experienced individual and collective healing and found wholeness.

• There are hymns which may be familiar to particular congregations which offer insights into the conditions for generativity e.g. *Just as I am* reminds Christians of the acceptance that they are promised in *Christ; Come thou fount of every blessing* includes the line 'Here I raise my Ebenezer' in some versions. This relates to 1 Samuel 7.12, when Samuel set down a marker to show how far God had helped the Israelites. Ebenezer means 'stone of help' – a reminder for congregations of their reliance on God.

• There are spiritual traditions which use imagination to make intuitive leaps forward in understanding God e.g. Julian of Norwich's *Revelations of Divine Love.*

- One church in Gloucestershire was convinced that an AI process couldn't help them because they were too few and too old. However, the practitioner asked them to think what small things they'd like to learn more about. Out of the ensuing discussion came the comment that, in their age-group, they'd like to share hope when people speak of ageing and death. Far from being pessimistic, the church felt that could be a real light in a culture that is still averse to voicing thoughts about mortality.

Biblical insights into generativity

"God saw everything that he had made and indeed, it was very good." Genesis 1.31

"Do not be conformed to this world, but be transformed by the renewing of your minds, so that you may discern what is the will of God – what is good and acceptable and perfect." Romans 12.2

Jesus engages with a conversation with the Samaritan woman at the well and their exchange leads to something new – her recognition of him as the Messiah. There is astonishment from his disciples that he should be talking with a woman, and her testimony spreads the word about him to an unexpected extent. An encounter generates newness in John 4.5-42.

AI Principles and Illustrations from *Appreciating Church*

Five core principles underpin all AI practice. These principles are woven into every stage of an AI process, and a process can't be considered 'truly AI' without considering each of them. The principles are: constructionist; simultaneity; anticipatory; poetic and positive. Each explanation that follows includes insights from the Bible and Church traditions, and an alternative name for each principle, based on a Bible story, has been included.

The Constructionist Principle:

Words create worlds
The constructionist principle is based on the theory of social constructionism, which proposes that our individual realities are formed by our interpretation and perception, which is different for each of us. Conceptually, it proposes that our reality at any given moment is formed by our interpretation and perception of what we experience, and that interpretation and perception will be different for each of us. We're constantly formed and reformed by the influences of our life experience, family, education, communities, work, beliefs, values, and what we witness.

"Reality is merely an illusion, albeit a very persistent one."

Albert Einstein

"We are in continuous conversations with each other and with ourselves. Through conversation we form and reform our life experiences and events; we create and recreate our meanings and understandings; and we construct and reconstruct our realities and ourselves. Some conversations enhance possibility; others diminish it."

Harlene Anderson

It is the application of this principle within AI that encourages people to expand their perception of reality and the range of possibilities that they can apply to their situation.

Key points:
- Words create worlds
- Multiple interpretations of what is real co-exist
- We're constantly co-creating our reality with every conversation and social interaction
- We create stories to make sense of things. Stories are not the truth, they are just one perspective and interpretation

Example:
Think of a typical Church occasion. Years later, the story is being retold and shared by various generations of people who were there – yet each person has a different view of what happened, and recounts a different version: who did and said what; what the outcome was; the detail of the occasion. Each participant will believe their story to be true.

Helpful hints:

- Notice the language you use and conversations you take part in, and how they impact on you and those around you
- Notice other people's language and images/metaphors in conversations
- Remember that each person's reality is subjective
- There is no right or wrong reality – just a difference of interpretation
- Remember – there are no neutral observers

"We do not see things as they are, we see them as we are." Anais Nin

"We are each made and imagined in the eyes of one another." David Cooperrider

The Constructionist Principle for the church: The Caesarea Philippi Principle

"Who do you say I am?" Matthew 16: 13-17

The constructionist principle tells us that people create stories to make sense of things. This rings bells with Christians, for whom the Bible is important as a means through which generations of believers have developed their understanding of God. Stories reveal the deeper truth of the divine. Truths are contextual, and who an individual understands Jesus to be will affect how they articulate their faith. Is he a social reformer, a spiritual guide, a prophet, the Messiah?

What Peter constructs for Jesus' identity is more complex, bringing in a wider pattern of experience than most people had had up to that point. Crucially, as Jesus makes clear in verse 17, this construct includes direct revelation from God as part of his understanding, and a whole new future is generated from it for all concerned.

There is a traditional way of engaging with the Bible which encourages imagining yourself as one of the characters, and understanding the story from their perspective – constructing an understanding based on how and what they would have seen. Two examples are given here briefly:

1. Four people lowered their paralysed friend through the roof of Jesus' home in Capernaum in order that he could be healed (Mark 2. 1-12). What did the crowd see and think? What other perspectives would the disciples or the scribes bring that would change the story for them?

2. At the wedding at Cana (John 2. 1-11), few of the characters involved knew the whole story, and most could only interpret events through a limited understanding: the steward only sees things relating to a generous host, while Mary had so much more to work from. While the servants may well have been giggling at all this, John encourages us to construct something much more significant with verse 11.

The Simultaneity Principle

The first question is fateful.

Simultaneity, the second of the core principles, recognises the fundamental reaction you set in motion by asking a question. It encourages you to take care in the crafting of questions and the choice of words, and to be aware of the impact they will have on different people, and the responses they might evoke.

"Change your questions, change your life." Marilee Adams

The first question you ask is fateful, so choose your words carefully. Beginning positively can be effective, e.g. stating how well a person looks or saying 'thank you for looking after me'.

Simultaneity reminds us that the language, tone and intention of the question determine the direction of the conversation – and that the moment we inquire, or ask a question, we initiate a reaction at many different levels of our consciousness.

Questions have an enormous capacity to create change. The way we craft and articulate our questions impacts on what people think, say and learn, and impacts on the dialogue which follows the question. When crafting our questions, we should be careful to make sure they are affirmative, rather than negative.

"Our understandings, beliefs and images evolve and change simultaneously as we seek to discover ourselves and the world through questions. There are no neutral questions – every inquiry takes us somewhere, even if it is back to what we originally believed. Inhabiting this spirit of wonder can transform our lives, and the unconditional positive question is one of the greatest tools we have to this end."

Jackie Kelm, Appreciative Living

An example:

You're about to meet up with an old friend – you're aware that their current life is complicated, with much going on, both good and bad. They have a new dream job involving lots of travel, but are also in the midst of a rocky personal relationship. You've had a long week and are hoping for a fun, energising evening.

Which direction are you hoping the conversation will focus on? Will it be stories of exciting new places, fulfilling and enriching work and a happy and bubbly old friend? Or stories of a dysfunctional relationship, moans about what's not working and difficult decisions to be made? The choice is yours! Remember, your first question is fateful...

'Reframing' is particularly relevant when applying this principle. It is the art of putting an affirmative frame around a topic which has been presented as a negative or deficit issue – so, when dealing with an issue of poor team working, for instance, it's helpful to look for examples of great teams for inspiration and guidance. Further discussion of reframing is given on page 91 of this resource.

Helpful hints:

- When you create your questions, consider what you're really seeking to learn more about, and how you can encourage the respondent to reflect on what is valuable;
- As the old adage goes, 'be careful what you wish for – you might just get it';
- Consider the path you'd like the dialogue to take. The moment you release a question, you have started your narrative journey;
- Try out your questions with a colleague to see how they interpret them. The way in which language is constructed can have different meanings for different people.

"Just when the caterpillar thought the world was over, it became a butterfly." Anon

One church in Market Harborough realised that its all-age service wasn't meeting the needs of anyone. The first assumption was that two services would be needed; one for older adults and one for families. However, one teenager at the church meeting spoke of how he valued everyone being together and how all the age groups came together over refreshments. This led to food-sharing becoming the heart of the worship. The meeting changed from, 'how can I get the worship I like?' to 'how can I make sure others can worship God in a way that works for them?'

The Simultaneity Principle for the Church:
The Emmaus Principle

What are you discussing with each other while you walk along? Luke 24.17

The Emmaus Road encounter is a wonderful example of the power of Appreciative Inquiry. The stranger asks a question which enables the two companions to tell their story and, in the process, interpret for themselves the experience they had undergone in the previous three days. In one interpretation Jesus challenges their thinking by saying … *How foolish you are, and how slow of heart to believe all that the prophets have spoken!* The conversation is so fruitful that they urge him to stay with them, and their recognition of Jesus in the breaking of the bread is in itself generative.

"What do you want me to do for you?" Mark 10.51, Matthew 20.32, Luke 18.41

In this story a blind man, begging at the side of the road, calls out to Jesus. In some ways it might be obvious what he might want from Jesus, but the question that Jesus asks opens up options for the answer.

Helpful practices

- Consider what experience you're seeking and how that could be assisted by the question you choose first.
- The wording of questions when offering authentic hospitality is important. 'Can you help me?' draws in new people more than 'can I help you?' Similarly a notice which says: 'welcome to your cathedral' has a different effect to 'welcome to X cathedral'. Is it possible to ask people 'what's the best welcome we could give you?' or 'what's the best welcome you've had?'
- Remember the Golden Rule of Matthew 7.12: *In everything do to others as you would have them do to you.*

The Anticipatory Principle:

Image inspires action

A cornerstone of AI practice, the anticipatory principle describes how we look forward and create ideas about what the future might hold for us. Our expectations and imagined scenarios lead us to make decisions that influence our present condition and actions. Our future is a constructed reality, created by present thinking and imagery. It's constantly influenced by our values, traditions, beliefs, assumptions and perceptions of what is possible, acceptable or desirable.

"Your imagination is your preview of life's coming attractions."   Albert Einstein

We all live in a future state to some extent, projecting, wondering and agonising over 'what will be'. Psychologists often distinguish humans from animals by our capacity for memory and imagination. Looking forward prompts us to make decisions which influence our present condition and actions. Positive visualisation is used both in many development models and in sports training. It is widely recognised that how we see possible futures inevitably influences the outcome.

Scientists have shown us that because positive and open mindsets produce exploration and experiential learning, they also come to produce more accurate mental maps of the world.

An example:

Think about an important event coming up; it could be an important church meeting or event, a presentation, or a family occasion. Whatever you've chosen, you'll be filled with anticipation; you'll have images that you project into the future of how the event could be. You could anticipate your future event with dread or loathing – fearing the worst, doubting your success and worrying about the possibility of things going wrong. Or you could anticipate your future event with love, tranquility, excitement and joy – imagining success and positive results. Our imagination is powerful and fuels our thoughts and actions – we choose what kinds of images we fill our heads with. By changing our images of the future, we can transform our future.

Helpful hints:

- When we create positive, uplifting images of our future – full of opportunity and possibility, whether personal or professional – we're more likely to make decisions and act to help us reach that desired future;

- If we constantly anticipate the worst, we fill ourselves with a sense of foreboding, fear and limitation;

- When we hold back on looking forward positively and embracing opportunity, we're sending a powerful message to our minds that whatever we're working towards isn't going to happen. This can prevent us from achieving our goals and stop us from feeling good in the meantime;

- We're constantly bombarded with negative images of life by the internet, media and people around us. This negativity bias can have a very unconscious influence on our thinking, so it is worth becoming more aware of it, and countering it. It's helpful to filter this and hold our own mental images of how and where we'd like to travel.

A Salvation Army corps was leaving its building to share premises with another local church. At first, they only saw losses and difficulties. However, during a tour of the new building they were invited to think of what good things could happen in the space. This led to a healthy balance between acknowledging, mourning and celebrating what happened in the old building and new hope for the future.

The Anticipatory Principle in the Church: Jeremiah's Field Principle

Biblical insights

At a time of crisis, when the Babylonian army was besieging Jerusalem and the people were facing deportation to exile, Jeremiah exercised his right to buy some family land at Anathoth. He did this in public view and with all the proper legalities, anticipating that there would come a day when land would again be bought by the rightful owners. Jeremiah 32

Jonah had a view of what would happen to Nineveh and became disgruntled when the outcome was not quite as he had expected. Jonah 4.1-5

Although Peter was initially able to create an idea of how he would emulate Jesus by walking on water, his realistic perception of what would normally be possible took over and he began to sink. Matthew 14. 22-33 (and also Mark 6. 45-53 and John 6 15-21).

Palm Sunday is an example of a crowd of people having a collective image of the kind of Messiah they were expecting, and fitting the present occurrence into their imagined future. Mark 11. 1-11, Matthew 21.1-11, Luke 19. 29-40, John 12.12-15.

Other insights:

- Teachers' expectations of students have a powerful affect;

- Applying this principle can help us include the possibility of doing unexpected/difficult things;

- The power of the placebo and nocebo[9] are illustrative of the anticipatory principle;

- There are particular films which draw on the power of imagined, anticipated or alternative futures like *Sliding Doors*, where a split second occurence has a huge impact on the protagonist's life. In *Life is Beautiful*, an Italian held in a wartime concentration camp protects his son from the horror of their lives by convincing him that they are involved in a game. *Field of Dreams* is based on the instruction, 'build it and they will come' and *Life of PI* offers alternative versions of what happens to a young man in a lifeboat.

"If we approach a thing saying: 'it can't be done' it will not, if we approach it by saying: 'it must be done', the chances are it will..."

William Barclay, in his Daily Study Bible on Luke 17 v.5-6

---

9   negative expectations can result in negative outcomes known as the *nocebo* effect

The Poetic Principle:

What we focus on grows

AI as a philosophy and a process for change relies heavily on an individual's narrative and vision of the future. We make sense of our lives through the stories we tell and hear, and what our imaginations lead us to aspire to and innovate to achieve. AI focuses on generating transformation and desired futures from discovered high points of learning and experience.

"A different language is a different vision of life." Federico Fellini

Writer Audre Lorde says: *'Poetry is not only dream and vision; it is the skeleton architecture of our lives. It lays the foundations for a future of change, a bridge across our fears of what has never been before.'*

There are a number of different interpretations of the poetic principle, but the following are what we've found useful.

Just as in a poem, hymn, prayer, reading, painting or piece of music, there are endless meanings, interpretations and significances, so there are in the stories that we hear and tell. We can find whatever we want to look for in any person, situation, organisation, or church. Each of us – either as an individual or part of a group – is an endless potential anthology of stories, pictures, images and narratives. Great poems, acts of worship, stories or art touch us on a number of sensory levels. The use of well-crafted evocative language or imagery allows us to tap into our own interpretations of thinking and feeling.

In Appreciative Inquiry we consciously focus on and seek out the stories of the experiences that we want more of.

"Human organisations are open books. An organisation's story is constantly being co-authored by people within the organisation as well as by those outside who interact with it... We can inquire into the nature of alienation or the nature of joy. We can study moments of creativity and innovation, or moments of debilitating stress. We have a choice."

Jane Magruder Watkins

An example:

Three men are chipping rock in a quarry. The first man is asked what he's doing, and replies that he is chipping rock. The second man is asked the same question, and says he's providing for his family. The final man, doing identical work, says that he is building a cathedral. If you're just chipping rock, you make yourself a common labourer; and while providing for your family gives you a personal purpose, finding the cathedral in your work can generate inspiration and motivation.

Helpful hints:

- What you focus on grows. In any moment we can choose to find bad, right, beautiful, ugly, perfection, imperfection, opportunity, or barriers;
- Be mindful of imposing your own assumptions and beliefs on what is positive, successful, and what matters;
- AI differs from positive thinking in that it's not about ignoring the challenges (see more about this on page 28), but is about making a conscious decision to put energy into what we want more of, and are already doing well. It is a conscious decision to find learning and something helpful and insightful in any situation.
- Deliberately choose provocative language that questions people on a more than everyday basis, and touches people at their core.

The Poetic Principle in the Church:

Lilies of the Field Principle

The idea of flowers weaving and sewing is ludicrous at one level, which is why this is an example of the poetic principle in action. Jesus' use of the metaphor lodges in the listener's mind and illustrates the point that is being made, as good poetry does. Matthew 6.28-30, Luke 12.27-28.

When the woman anointed Jesus' feet with perfume, did the aroma linger all week? Each of the Gospel writers include the basic story and give it a different subtle purpose within their overall account. In each case there is a sense of making a moment beautiful and a strong point emerges from it: Luke 7.36-38, Matthew 26.6-13, Mark 14.3-9, John 12.1-8.

What's important here is imagination, and that's apparent in other practices of the church:

- *Lecto Divina* in which a biblical text is allowed to be absorbed by hearing, reading and slow contemplation, so that its meaning in the moment is revealed.
- The symbols at the heart of many rituals such as the breaking of bread and pouring of wine in communion.
- The words of hymns which often start from, yet go beyond, biblical texts and images. For instance, *O for a thousand tongues to sing; I heard the voice of Jesus say; The Servant King*
- Using art work – which may or may not have a specifically religious theme – as part of the environment or focus of worship.

The Positive Principle:

Positive questions lead to positive change

The positive principle challenges us to look at and articulate when we feel positive, vibrant, vital, and empowered; when we – as individuals, communities and organisations – are at our best; when we are exceptional and shine.

"Positive images of the future are a powerful and magnetic force. They draw us on and energise us, give us courage and will to take important initiatives. Negative images of the future also have magnetism – they pull the spirit downward on the path of despair and impotence."

William James, 1842-1910

Positive emotions and attitudes lead to positive action. Positive psychology and wellbeing research has long established that a positive outlook contributes to our health, wellbeing, resilience and optimal functioning. Over the last ten years, more attention has been paid to differentiating and understanding a broad range of positive emotions.

"Positive emotions are not trivial luxuries but instead might be critical necessities for optimal functioning."

Barbara Frederickson

A helpful way to see how negativity can effect individuals and groups is the 'negativity bias' concept – the phenomena by which humans give more psychological weight to bad experiences than good ones. Some researchers assert that negative emotions have an impact close to three times stronger than positive emotions.

Often, 'bad stuff' is stronger than 'good stuff'. You think about bad experiences for longer periods of time, and they weigh more heavily upon you.

"Momentum and change requires large amounts of positive effect and social bonding – things like hope, excitement, inspiration, caring, camaraderie, sense of urgent purpose and sheer joy in creating something meaningful together."

David Cooperrider and Diana Whitney, *A Positive Revolution in Change*

These are a few helpful hints on minimising negativity bias:

- **Awareness:** Be aware that your body is caught up with emotions of anxiety and fear. Once you have recognised it you're more likely to react strongly to negative stimuli in you environment.
- **Be mindful:** Allow yourself time to stop and think about the whole picture before reacting to a given situation. When you face a negative event make sure you take time to reflect and think before you react.
- **Enjoy:** When something positive happens, pause and enjoy the feeling for several moments.
- **Self-compassion:** Take care of yourself and your relationships. Make sure you give yourself and your relationships an abundance of opportunities to experience the positive.

"Positive people are able to maintain a broader perspective and see the big picture which helps them identify solutions, whereas negative people maintain a narrower perspective and tend to focus on problems."

Barbara Frederickson

Barbara Fredrickson's **broaden and build** theory states that positive emotions play an essential role in our wellbeing. Positive emotions, like love, joy, and gratitude, promote new and creative actions, ideas, and social bonds. When people experience positive emotions, their minds **broaden** and they open up to new possibilities and ideas, it helps people **build** their personal well-being resources – physical, intellectual and social.

"Positivity opens us. The first core truth about positive emotions is that they open our hearts and our minds making us more receptive and more creative."

Barbara Fredrickson

Positive emotions:

- broaden thinking and repertoire of reactions
- build resilience and upward spirals
- support physical wellbeing

"The highest success in living and the deepest emotional satisfaction comes from building and using your signature strengths."

Martin Seligman, Authentic Happiness

AI aims to establish the positive core of a person, organisation, or community. It inquires into this core to find what we are proud of and do best. AI looks at key strengths and attributes that enable us to be resilient, open to learning and able to take action in a positive direction.

Some critics consider this 'Pollyanna' thinking (from a children's book where the character Pollyanna plays 'the glad game', looking for good in every situation.) Others criticise the positive thinking movement, labelling it as naïve or unrealistic optimism. However AI doesn't ignore the challenges or the reality of any given situation. Instead of focusing energy on the problem by asking 'what isn't working?' or 'what are we doing wrong?'; we ask 'when are we at our best?' 'what do we do really well?'and 'how could we be even better?'

In *Appreciative Inquiry. Change at the Speed of Imagination*, Jane Magruder Watkins and Ralph Kelly remind us that sometimes the answer to the AI question, 'tell me a story about your best experience.' can begin with a story about some unpleasant and difficult time – but go on to describe how the storyteller managed well, learned from it, and now considers it a 'best experience'.

Examples – which of the following questions gives you more energy?

- What are the weaknesses that you need to work on? *OR*
- What are your strengths that you can develop further?
- What's happening in this church/congregation to create low morale? *OR*
- What's happening here when we are at our best and fulfilling God's mission?

Helpful hints:

- Appreciative Inquiry is the cousin of positive psychology;
- Read the in-depth work of Martin Seligman and Barbara Fredrickson;
- Appreciative journaling helps us explore and practice the positive principle (see page 99).

The Positive Principle in the Church:

The fig tree principle

"Then he told this parable: 'A man had a fig tree planted in his vineyard; and he came looking for fruit on it and found none. So he said to the gardener, "See here! For three years I have come looking for fruit on this fig tree, and still I find none. Cut it down! Why should it be wasting the soil?" He replied, "Sir, let it alone for one more year, until I dig around it and put manure on it. If it bears fruit next year, well and good; but if not, you can cut it down."'"
Luke 13.6-9

The positive principle seeks out the essential goodness or value in a person, relationship, community, congregation or project. The parable of the fig tree suggests that it is worth being patient and persistent as well as giving organisations the support they need in order to flourish and bear fruit. Being positive as a Christian is much more about trusting in God and holding to a perspective of generosity than adherence to 'positive thinking'. It is the Christian understanding of hope in God that makes the difference.

Biblical insights

Is our view of God as positive as it can be? Is it based on hope?

"The steadfast love of the Lord never ceases, his mercies never come to an end; they are new every morning; great is your faithfulness." Lamentations 3.22-23

"But immediately Jesus spoke to them and said 'Take heart, it is I; do not be afraid.' Peter answered him, 'Lord, if it is you, command me to come to you on the water.' He said, 'Come'. So Peter got out of the boat, started walking on the water, and came toward Jesus." Matthew 14.27-29

"May the God of hope fill you with all joy and peace in believing, so that you may abound in hope by the power of the Holy Spirit." Romans 15.13

"We are afflicted in every way, but not crushed; perplexed, but not driven to despair; persecuted, but not forsaken; struck down, but not destroyed; always carrying in the body the death of Jesus, so that the life of Jesus may also be made visible in our bodies." 2 Corinthians 4.8-10

"Always be ready to make your defence to anyone who demands from you an account of the hope that is in you; yet do it with gentleness and reverence." 1 Peter 3. 15b-16a (as part of advice to people who may be persecuted for being Christian)

"But those who wait for the Lord shall renew their strength, they shall mount up with wings like eagles, they shall run and not be weary, they shall walk and not faint." Isaiah 41.4

Other insights

"Faith is having a positive attitude about what you can do, not worrying about what you can't do."
Participant at the AI and the Churches consultation, March 2016

"When I was about seven years old, I announced that my favourite text was 'Hitherto hath the Lord helped me'. The elders were amused, but I am not so sure that it was funny after all. The distance from one birthday to the next seems infinite to a small child, and 'the thoughts of youth are long, long thoughts'. Looking back over many years, I fancy my choice now would be much the same. I am not prepared, here and now, to analyse and define the reasons, but I can only say that this quiet certainty has run all through my life linking up babyhood and youth and middle age with the latest stretch of the road and 'hitherto', though sometimes almost slipping through one's fingers, that golden thread has never wholly escaped my grasp."
Elizabeth Fox Howard, 1943; Quaker faith & practice 21.02

"Keep your thoughts positive because your thoughts become your words. Keep your words positive because your words become your behaviour. Keep your behaviour positive because your behaviour becomes your habits. Keep your habits positive because your habits become your values. Keep your values positive because your values become your destiny."
Mohandas Karamchand Gandhi

"It is imperative that we maintain hope even when the harshness of reality may suggest the opposite."
Paulo Freire

The hymn *Best of all is God is with us* by Andrew Pratt draws on the words of John Wesley: http://gbod.org.s3.amazonaws.com/legacy/kintera/entry_13815/66/bestofallis-pratt.pdf

The Emergent Principles

As AI practitioners have refined their learning and experience (in keeping with AI philosophy) some 'emergent principles' have been added. *Appreciative Living: the principles of AI in personal life*, by Jackie Kelm, provides an excellent summary of these.

They sit alongside the core principles, although some practitioners prefer to see them as 'intentions' for the work, rather than principles. Three of these emergent principles are:

* The wholeness principle – focusing on wholeness brings out the best, brings everyone together, builds collective capacity;
* The enactment principle – walk the talk, be the change you want to see, model the future you are aiming for;
* The awareness principle – be as aware as possible of our own inner processes and those of other people.
* Further information on these emergent principles can be found on the website: www.appreciating.church

Hillsborough – using the AI principles

Here is an example from Suzanne Nockels of both the social construction and positive principles in action. Hillsborough is an area in Sheffield, South Yorkshire, which was the scene of a major tragedy in April 1989 when 96 people were killed and 766 injured during a football match between Liverpool and Nottingham Forest. The tragedy was compounded by the way its causes were covered up, and it was only in 2016 that the truth was fully recognised and justice begun to be realised. It is a clear example of how words create worlds, multiple interpretations exist and how the AI principles can interrelate.

When we hear the word Hillsborough, many people think immediately of the football disaster. So, when a new minister moved to Hillsborough Tabernacle Congregational Church, she felt that the local community needed to see its strengths, as well as understand the disaster that had taken place there. In particular, they wanted to be seen as a community which was more than the external negative perception of the Hillsborough label. Together the church used a big anniversary year to explore the theme of hope. It made artwork, it invited speakers including the local member of parliament, David Blunkett, to share their thoughts, it held music concerts and children's activities. It hosted a massive history fair celebrating the area that over a thousand people visited. The year has given the church fuel for the future and it's now embarking on a project to help people claim the benefits they are entitled to. After reflecting on hope they want to share it.

AI conversations/ interviews – developing questions and protocols

Appreciative interviews are at the heart of the AI philosophy. Often they're the most important part of the AI process. AI principles are central to crafting great, generative questions.

"There is no more powerful way to initiate significant change than to convene a conversation."

Margaret Wheatley

AI interviews, sometimes called appreciative conversations, can be used in many parts of an AI process. Essentially, they are a structured conversation, and normally called protocols – a useful bit of jargon. 'Protocol' is the term AI practitioners use to describe the sequence and focus of the questions. Sometimes just one really good question can make a significant difference, but a protocol usually varies in length from three to six questions, with the questioners being reminded to practice active listening. The value of a protocol is in encouraging deeper dialogue.

AI conversations, whether in the Church or elsewhere, focus on what's good, positive, what worked and how you felt about it. They generally prompt a new insight as the speaker reflects.

Good questions:
- are surprising
- touch peoples' heart and soul
- encourage sharing and listening to stories and experiences that enhance relationships
- cause us to look at reality a little differently

Tips for interviews:

- Use the protocol as your script – it's OK to change some of the language, just don't lose the meaning;
- It's helpful to ask supplementary questions like: 'who else was involved?', 'how did it make you feel?' and 'why did it work?';
- It's fine to miss a question and then go back later – some people find the process challenging and need time to respond;
- Be a great listener. Let the interviewee tell his/her story – please don't tell yours, nor give opinions or go off at tangents. It's very easy to do!;
- In your notes capture key words, themes and quotes, and listen for great stories;
- Be genuinely curious; allow for silence and thinking time.

Examples of 'open' questions that can be useful in many situations, and are worth keeping ready to use:

- What would be the best thing to do now?
- Given no constraints, what would you do?
- What is great about what you do?
- So what will you do that will work?
- What is the best question I could ask?
- What do we need to do differently?
- What is the smallest thing, and/or the most innovative thing, that would make a difference?
- Isn't that interesting? Tell me more...

Helpful hints in designing and using protocols:

- Sometimes all you need is one really good question rather than a whole protocol e.g. What is the best possible outcome from this meeting?;
- Use the term 'appreciative conversation' if the word 'interview' could alienate people – this might be especially useful in community settings;
- Allocate plenty of time to craft and pilot questions (try them out first with a friendly listener);
- Use a variety of formats like social media and group interviews – it's about what works in the culture;
- You will know the right questions to ask;
- Protocols are great at the definition stage, or to give people a simple AI experience
- The simultaneity and poetic principles (which you'll find on pages 23 and 26) are very evident in these conversations.

"If we were meant to talk MORE and listen LESS we would have two mouths and one ear."
Mark Twain

Appreciative conversations are normally paired conversations, but they can also be carried out in a group. Creating protocols and designing questions is, in some ways, an art form, and takes practise.

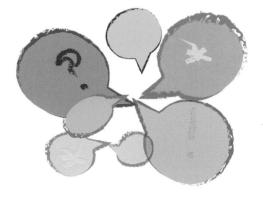

Example of a fairly standard protocol:

Q1:   Share a story about a time or experience when you were proud of what you achieved and when you've made a difference. What was successful about it and what did you achieve?

Q2:   Describe your top five strengths and share an example in your present role of when you've successfully used one.

Q3:   What are the things you value deeply: specifically, the things you value about yourself and the successful things you've done?

Q4:   We're meeting on this day next year and reviewing the progress this organisation (or community/ network/ church) has made. What would be its successes, what would be different and how have the challenges been resolved?

Q5:   (a): What are one small step and one large step that could be taken by the organisation that would make a difference?

   (b): An alternative to this question is: 'what are your three wishes?'

Alternatively, a protocol can be just three questions on one side of a postcard (the other side could have positive images of the church), such as:

1. What do you value about being part of this church community?

2. What one small thing and one big thing would you change to make a difference?

3. What are you already doing to support this church and its community? (It can be something tiny).

Helpful hints:

• Encourage story telling and sharing of experience. Narratives are powerful;

• Collect protocols – adapting from existing good practice saves time;

• When asking the questions be prepared for people who want to stay with the problems and be negative. Allow them some space, rather than close it down – try and help people to see the learning, or notice elements that demonstrated strength and resilience;

• In some places the 'three wishes' question (Q5b) is a great question; in others it is a turn off. Find out what works for you and your situation;

• Protocols have a rhythm and flow – opening questions encourage stories and sharing of experience, later ones cover topics and intent;

• You'll know it's a good protocol when people say: 'wow – that's an interesting question';

• Conversations will vary in length but be prepared for them overrunning;

• Remember the AI principles (pages 21-30);

• Respect what people tell you and check out with them what can be shared in subsequent stages of group conversations.

"When you are listening to somebody, completely, attentively, then you are listening not only to the words, but also to the feeling of what is being conveyed, to the whole of it, not part of it."

Jiddu Krishnamurti

"In true dialogue, both sides are willing to change."

Thich Nhat Hanh

You'll find further information and guidance on AI questions and protocols in parts three and four of this resource and on the website: www.appreciating.church.

Introduction to the 5D cycle

The 5D process is one of the AI core tools and is a useful framework for designing protocols, projects, and a whole range of AI interventions from the personal to the large scale and organisation-wide. The 5D cycle is one of the core tools within AI and is often thought of (incorrectly, as it happens) as what AI is all about. However, it is very useful as a mechanism to deliver AI. It has been adapted from time to time – the Village Banks organisation in Nepal, for instance, has a 7D cycle with two additions after destiny: 'do it' and 'dance and drum' (to celebrate success).

In the descriptions below, you will find guidance on activities you can use and helpful hints to support you through the process. They are based on the creation of a church development plan. The St Bride's story (page 68) will also help you further understand the process.

The 5D cycle is now in common usage and this 5D drawing shows how the 5Ds relate to each other.

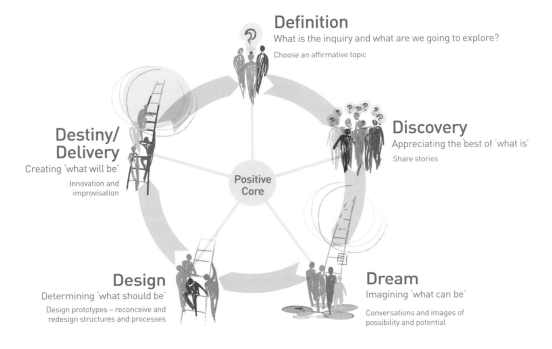

Definition
What is the inquiry and what are we going to explore?
Choose an affirmative topic

Discovery
Appreciating the best of 'what is'
Share stories

Destiny/Delivery
Creating 'what will be'
Innovation and improvisation

Positive Core

Dream
Imagining 'what can be'
Conversations and images of possibility and potential

Design
Determining 'what should be'
Design prototypes – reconceive and redesign structures and processes

"Defining and discovering my dream enables me to design my own destiny."

Participant on an AI course

D for Definition: What is the inquiry and what are we going to explore?

"Off by an inch in the beginning, off by ten thousand miles at the end."

Master Hsuan Hua

Originally, AI was based on the 4D cycle (discover, dream, design and destiny) developed in Zimbabwe as part of an international development programme. Definition is a more recent addition, and is valuable in clarifying the area of work to be considered. Therefore the 5D model has become standard AI practice.

Definition identifies the project purpose, content, and what needs to be achieved. Essentially it involves choosing the right area to inquire into. It is about making sure that you're getting to the heart of the issue. Exploring and defining the initial issue often reveals something else to be more fundamental. Defining the inquiry topic positively ensures the process can move in a generative direction. Reframing is a useful skill here (see page 91).

Guidelines for the 'definition' stage:

- It should stretch and challenge the status quo;
- Be open minded: actions that follow may be unexpected;
- Stay outcome-focused (which can be ill-defined in the early stages). Allow for development and refinement as you go along;
- It's all about positive phrasing – language that will engage and excite people;
- From the start, involve as many people as possible across the organisation;
- The topic selection should excite, be provocative, and encourage dialogue.

Helpful hints:

- Remember – the initial proposal is often not the real task. Be open to change and redefinition, and take the time needed;
- Try and ensure, as much as possible, that there is a 'buy in' at the highest level;
- Encourage flexibility and adaptability in this stage, and encourage review throughout the process;
- Be prepared for outcomes to change as you go along;
- Look out for the 'oblique' effect – the generative nature of AI can produce additional positive outcomes alongside the identified task; capture these!
- Work with the group to agree the protocol questions, test them and finalise the process;
- Seek group support throughout the project and use them to provide feedback on the journey through the process.

How to do definition:

- Assemble a core group to support the project and provide local advice and information. The group can also undertake the appreciative conversations if they are being undertaken prior to a church planning day.
- Support includes defining the inquiry theme, the people to be involved, the process and outline outcomes.
- Introduce the core group to AI either by running an *Introduction to AI workshop* or, at a minimum, with experience of an AI conversation and reflection on its impact. This is essential as it gives people an opportunity to experience an AI process.
- If the 5D cycle is being used in a team or individual setting, start the process with an appreciative conversation as it will help the creation of the inquiry.

Creating a core group will help definition and some AI training for them will support their understanding. In *Appreciative Inquiry in Higher Education* (2012) Jeanie Cockell and Joan McArthur Blair set out the 'appreciative climate' they established to co-write their book. The agreements they made can be very helpful to support a core group's role:

- Ask brilliant questions of each other's work;
- Create and honour structure, deadlines and outcomes;
- Play and be creative to bubble up the energy;
- Appreciate your differences;
- Deeply listen to feedback;
- Care for yourselves and each other.

Examples of possible definitions for inquiries:

Creating a thriving and supportive spiritual community – a place for spiritual growth
Creating Our Future Together: Reimagining St Bride's

D for Discovery: appreciating the best of 'what is'

Discovery is the second stage of the 5D cycle. It's essentially based on dialogue and structured conversations. By considering 'what works' in depth, it rediscovers and remembers the organisation or community's successes, strengths, and periods of excellence.

"At its best, Appreciative Inquiry is serious, deliberate, rigorous research into the root causes of success."

David Cooperrider

Discovery can be seen as having three elements:

1. AI conversations and interviews explore the strengths, skills and capabilities of individuals, communities and organisations, and focus on the high points. This phase is normally conducted through paired conversations, although in some cultures this stage is conducted in groups. (See page 87 for discussion of appreciative conversation/ interview.)
2. Capturing the interview information by identifying the key ideas, stories and experiences, and clustering them into themes for use in subsequent 5D stages.
3. Identifying and naming the 'positive core' which provides a foundation for the next stages.

The positive core:

- All people, organisations and experiences have a positive core, however small it may be
- The positive core consists of strengths, achievements, opportunities, wisdom, unexplored potential and assets
- The positive core expands as it is affirmed and appreciated. Building strengths is more effective than correcting weaknesses

"Man cannot discover new oceans unless he has the courage to lose sight of the shore."

Andre Gide

"For listening to the stories of others... is a kind of water that breaks the fever of our isolation. If we listen closely enough, we are soothed into remembering our common name."

Mark Nepo

How to do discovery

There are usually two steps to this phase: the first step is a paired conversation and the second step is sharing stories in small groups and undertaking a series of tasks to identify emerging common themes.

Step one

Move people into pairs, suggesting they choose someone they know least, or would like to know more about. Go through the questions and interview guidance. If there is an odd number, one group of three will work but allocate extra time. Encourage people to find a comfortable place to talk.

Here's an example protocol (see the explanation of this term on page 31 (example) and further examples on pages 33, 83, 87 and 90)

1. Think of a time or experience when your involvement and engagement with this church has made a difference.
2. How would you describe your involvement in this church community?
3. How does this church community support and feed your spiritual life? It can be the smallest thing.
4. What is special about this place and the people involved?
5. In your experience what does this church community do really well?
6. What do you think needs to be done differently?
7. It is spring 2022 and we are meeting to celebrate our journey together. What has been achieved and what is different? What are the challenges that have been overcome? Describe it as if it has happened.
8. What could help move things on? What's one small step and one innovative one?

Note how the questions mirror elements of the 5D process. The answers and responses provide information for step two. You can do the appreciative conversations in avariety of ways: prior to the planning day so that people are engaged; in a group; and during the planning day. Be flexible.

Step two

After the paired conversation, move into groups of four to six (or large groups of eight to ten when dealing with big gatherings) and give each group their tasks, allocating them one at a time.

Sequence of tasks:

1. Ask each person to share their story or experience. This can be done by the listener, the teller or a mixture. This is an important stage and should not be missed.
2. Discuss and then draw up a list of the ways this church feeds and supports people's spiritual life.
3. Discuss and co-create a list of why your church and its people are special.
4. Discuss and co-create a list of what your church does well.
5. Discuss and co-create a list of things your church needs to do differently
6. List the small and innovative steps.

After discussion, each task is recorded on a flip chart and, at the end of the process, shared in a plenary session. One way this can be done easily is for one group to start with their list and the following groups add to the list. Or place the flip charts on a wall so the facilitator can highlight the key points. The lists are used as a resources for the other phases. The dream question (No.7 in the first list) is there to help the thinking process at the dream stage. You may not have time to do all the tasks, so choose the most important.

Helpful hints:

- The discovery stage can be an exciting and uplifting and there will often be emotional and 'light bulb' moments;
- Don't rush to the next stage – allocate plenty of time;
- Emphasise the importance of sharing the story or experience;
- Remember that children and some cultures may struggle with paired conversations. Use a group conversation with each person answering the question in turn. A talking stick is great for this.
- Take time to explain the process, the questions and feedback arrangements, including how the information will be used for the next phases ;
- Your protocols need to be challenging and to elicit relevant stories and experiences;
- Involve as many people as possible in the process of gathering the themes that emerge;
- Share the conversation and discovered stories in a group – it helps foster generativity;
- It can be useful to record the stories in either film or book format, or use social media;
- This stage can look a bit messy – that's fine!
- Remember the core AI principles – the constructionist, simultaneity, and positive principles are particularly relevant at this stage.
- Try not to share the later questions before the conversations as it can often restrict spontaneity.
- Note the question sequence mirrors the 5D model, as this helps with all the stages;
- Generative ideas and metaphors begin to emerge – look out for them. They will seem to hold a lot of energy for people and keep being talked about. They will result in people discovering a fresh perspective on something in the inquiry and/ or the organisation. Even at this stage people may identify new and different actions they want to take – be ready to capture these.
- Don't ignore the negative – just try and look at things from a different angle. Task five will provide you with the challenges and issues, but in a different way.

D is for dream: imagining 'what can be'

"Martin Luther King didn't say 'I have a strategic plan'; instead he shouted 'I have a dream', and he created a movement."

Anon

Dream is the third stage of the 5D cycle, providing the opportunity for people to identify their dreams for the community and organisation. Having first discovered 'what is best' from past achievements and successes, they now have the chance to project it into their wishes, hopes and aspirations, to imagine new possibilities and envisage a preferred future. See how the 5Ds fit together on page 43.

Guidelines for the dream stage:

- The dream phase is highly practical as it's grounded in the organisation or group's history (rather than being unbounded vision making);
- The aim of the process is to amplify the positive core and to stimulate a more energised and inspirational future;
- It's important to foster creativity, imagery, metaphor, and 'passionate thinking'. Encourage people to think and act differently and outside of their comfort zone. If you're facilitating the process provide art and collage materials and a variety of play and creative opportunities;
- The dream stage helps to foster generativity (see page 19).

"Dreams pass into the reality of action. From the actions stems the dream again; and this interdependence produces the highest form of living."

Anais Nin

Some men see things as they are and say, 'Why?' Others dream of things that never were and say, 'Why not?'"

George Bernard Shaw

How to move into dream

Continue to use the small groups from step two of the discovery phase and set them a task to present their dream phase. A useful way to introduce this is:

It is three years' time and we've come together to celebrate our achievements and journey to this place. Each group is tasked with presenting the journey to this point. What has been achieved, what challenges were overcome and what work was completed?

Encourage participants to present as if things have happened. Use terms like: 'we did this'; 'these challenges were overcome' and 'we learned from this and did these things differently'.

We usually allocate up to 45 minutes, and then ask the small groups to present to the wider group.

Helpful hints

- As the dreams are based on the definition and discovery phases they should be based on reality and shared history. Encourage people to use all the data collected and shared in the discovery phase
- Do not be surprised if people take time to get going
- Introduce this phase by reminding people that Martin Luther King did not have a strategic plan – he had a dream
- Some people might struggle with dream. In this case use the term 'back planning'. It comes from the military and it is basically planning from the position of having achieved the outcome and describing the actions required to achieve this.
- If children are present they may also struggle with the dream phase, as thinking years ahead can be a challenge. Use the idea of being in Dr Who's TARDIS or waking up from a long sleep such as the Rip Van Winkle fairy story.

- Encourage people to present back their dreams in a variety of ways. This activity can be fun – don't be surprised when you get poetry, drama and dance. Support people to move away from the flip chart presentation. You will be surprised what will emerge – it is often playful and fun!
- Build up a store of play and arts suppliers – people love playing.
- Give plenty of time to prepare and provide time for presentations.
- Go around the small groups and encourage them.
- Use appreciative feedback (page 101) and encourage people to notice the ideas and suggestions from other group dream presentation- a source of additional ideas
- Remember the principles (pages 21-30) and refer back if necessary
- People can get a lot out of listening to each other's dreams. Display and possibly film the dreams, as they'll help in the design stage.
- Remember that the 5D process is not just circular – you can do mini cycles at each stage.

D is for design: determining 'what should be'

The design stage is where the stories and the best work from discovery are brought together with the imagination and creativity from the dream stage. This creates the structures and working arrangements to move things forward, bringing the 'best of what is' together with 'what might be' to create 'what should be – the ideal'.

Design is the fourth stage of the 5D cycle, where the emerging themes identified in the previous stages are developed into provocative propositions (see page 44). Provocative propositions are developed as signposts and intentions to support the structures and systems needed for a successful destiny phase.

Guidelines for the design stage:

For many AI practitioners, this stage requires real effort and the most rewarding work can be done. For the participant, it's where the real challenges emerge and there may be resistance. Recent experience has pinpointed three important influences for the design stage:

- Learn from the fields of product design and architecture – bring ideas and concepts to life by creating models, structures and different ways to do them;
- Use 'prototyping' ideas and methods developed within the product design world; Recognise that a product may go through a number of prototypes, often failing at the first stage and requiring a rethink. That's how the best products emerge and are successful;
- 'Say yes to the mess' – AI thinker Frank Barrett's useful advice. Learn from jazz music to constantly improvise and create structures that are adaptable and flexible.

How to do design:

In this phase, the groups who worked on the dream phase discuss and agree a short provocative proposition/forward statement. This is shared in plenary, and the large group discuss and agree a set of development tasks.

Helpful hints:

- Remember, this is about designing the process and social architecture, not about doing it.
- Encourage small groups with defined actions. To help the design process, set up small groups with a defined timeframe who can collaborate on a topic.
- A recent participant on an *Appreciating Church* training course referred to this stage as 'constructing the scaffolding'
- Remember that AI differs from other vision and forward thinking methodologies. It supports future working arrangements which are grounded in existing strengths, success and skills. This stage can be hard work – it can and will challenge historic practice and embedded cultures, and may meet resistance.
- Use AI protocols (see page 31) to explore ideas and different approaches.
- Engage the whole system – the full group often have great ideas and practical suggestions.
- Encourage developing and creating prototypes – and avoid pilot projects.

- Remember – churches and communities are learning ones!
- SOAR™ is very useful at this point – see page 45.
- Avoid the tendency to rush to delivery/destiny. The design stage is essential.
- Remember the principles and the importance of generativity.

"Managers should act not only as decision makers, but also as designers."

R.J. Boland, Jr. and F. Collopy

Prototyping

Alongside the SOAR™ model and the intention description below, a recent AI development in the design stage is the use of prototyping. It is important to differentiate prototyping from developing a pilot model. Within the design stage, developing a prototype can be the creation of a team or process to create a fully functioning and operational model. A church-based example of this is work begun in April 2016 by the United Reformed Church Yorkshire Synod to co-create and co-design a new Church Life Review system. Working with a number of churches across the Synod a working prototype is being developed, tested and adapted before going operational across the URC. As soon as it is completed the story of its development will be placed on the *Appreciating Church* website.

D for delivery/ destiny: creating 'what will be'

This fifth stage of the 5D cycle builds on the dream and design process to create arrangements for delivery/destiny. The previous stages defined the inquiry, and the design phase co-created and co-designed the structures, tasks and supportive working relationships that emerged from the previous three stages. This fifth stage identifies how it's delivered and embedded into groups, communities and organisations.

"Visions without tasks are just a dream; tasks without visions are pure drudgery; but put tasks to visions and you can change the world."

Chief Black Elk of the Oglala Sioux

Delivery/ destiny is the fifth stage of the 5D cycle. Called delivery in early AI development, it was based on more traditional organisational development practices like action planning, strategies and implementation plans. Recently, the term destiny has become more prevalent, recognising that the preceding process has created a climate for those things to happen organically, and a key element of destiny is to support this process.

Guidelines for the destiny stage:

- One of the dictionary definitions of destiny is 'the predetermined or inevitable course of events';
- The purpose of this stage is to sustain momentum so groups, individuals and organisations can build capacity to keep doing the work. It builds on the positive energy, creativity, and co-design developed in the earlier stages. This is often called 'maintaining an appreciative eye';
- Say 'yes to the mess' and accept that transformation requires improvisation, adaptability, and flexibility;
- This is where the prototypes, structures and models created in the design stage are presented and implemented;
- Remember Dwight D Eisenhower's words: *"Plans are nothing; planning is everything"*;
- AI evidence suggests that momentum for change and long-term sustainability increases when conventional implementation arrangements, like formal action planning, and monitoring progress are used sparingly – instead encourage innovation and foster learning and reflection.

Intentions as an alternative to plans – information and guidance

So do you have an intention for your church, or do you have a plan? Perhaps you have neither, of course. The only challenge with neither is that it is very easy to get distracted with tempting opportunities that may lead to you never completing anything, not following up with someone, or ending up wandering around with no sense of accomplishment or purpose. Not that that is bad, of course, but it may be somewhat dissatisfying. The concept of 'intentions' and its use in leadership[10] and in the 5D cycle is an interesting alternative to more traditional views on leadership and planning.

The work of David Marquet on intent-based leadership is helpful here:

"Leadership should mean giving control rather than taking control, and creating leaders rather than forging followers. Communities are built by volunteers who choose to do their work for free. The rules for building a community are the opposite of those in old-fashioned organisations. Instead of telling people what to do, spend time talking about intent."

David Marquet, from *Turn The Ship Around!* or: *True Story of Building Leaders by Breaking the Rules,* 2013

It's not about having a plan and sticking to it. It's about having an intention. A successful leader recognises the chaos, lack of a complete information picture, changes in a situation, and other relevant factors that may make a plan completely or partially obsolete when it is executed. The role of a successful leader is to emancipate others and guide their initiative and improvisation as they adapt a plan to a changing environment.

'Emancipation is fundamentally different from empowerment. You know you have an emancipated team when you no longer need to empower them... they are not relying on your as their source of power,' says Marquet.

Such a leader is vital in chaotic, demanding, and dynamic environments. A traditional planning approach with aims and objectives with a fixed timescale can be quickly out of date and too limiting. However, **an intention allows for flexibility, clarity of purpose and simplicity.** Keep intentions simple, clear and flexible. If you can say it one sentence all the better – it can always be expanded upon.

How many Church plans are unrealistically detailed and formulaic? Or are not relevant to the changing realities and sit on a shelf gathering dust? They may have been made by the few and not involved all the voices. The intention approach provides a planning framework that fits well with an AI approach of co-designing and co- creating at the design and destiny stages. It is flexible and adaptable and can include detailed plans when required which clearly meet the intention.

Here are three helpful hints when using the intention approach:

- Any action or plan that does not meet the intention is not undertaken;
- Review intentions periodically to check if they are still relevant;
- Create action plans that have short delivery timescales that are achievable.

How to move into destiny/ delivery

Using the format provided on page 36, small groups can discuss and then write down the actions and or steps. Using Post-it notes helps, as they can be moved around easily. After the groups have completed this task, share in plenary the ideas and then prioritise them.

Action plans are useful at this stage and the model below offers a user-friendly format for identifying next steps. For some people action plans are helpful and should not be ignored as a possible useful tool. The titles can be changed if appropriate to **'no money,' 'some money'** and **'abundance'**. Use a large flip chart for the model and write down the actions on Post-it notes so that they can be easily moved around and grouped. Then use task and finish groups to help deliver the actions, remembering to feed back the achievements and progress to sustain engagement.

---

10   When creating intentions for an organisation, group or church, substitute a term that works for you word in place of 'leader'.

Identify the actions to be taken now, sooner, and later in the relevant column.

Now	Sooner	Later

Helpful hints:

- In some situations an action plan will work and people may feel more comfortable with it, but try and wean them off it. Support the creation of intentions;
- Encourage people to create plans around simple and radical steps;
- Tiny changes can make a real difference;
- Remember, this is about maintaining momentum and leadership at all levels in the organisation and engaging personal commitment;
- Get people to sign up to their actions and personal commitments;
- Look for examples of generativity (page 19) and illustrations of the principles at work;
- Ensure there is 'buy in' across the congregation, organisation, group or community, and that they 'own' the solutions;
- Identify the small steps and celebrate when they're achieved;
- Remember the process is circular – and something new to inquire into may emerge during this phase.

Keep in mind when addressing the 5Ds...

Helpful hints have been given for each of the 5Ds above. The following apply to any part of the cycle:

- Use paired conversations and protocols at all stages;
- Be patient and let the process flow;
- Go back to definition and discovery in design and destiny/delivery if it helps clarify thinking;
- Remember to stay flexible and be adaptable;
- A one-day event will potentially get beyond the dream phase, be able to achieve provocative propositions and identify some actions for the design and destiny/delivery phases. These later phases can be done as either a second church-wide event and/or series of task and finish groups with specific functions and report back system.
- Don't forget to celebrate success and review impact.

"Our life is composed greatly from dreams, from the unconscious, and they must be brought into connection with action. They must be woven together."

Anais Nin

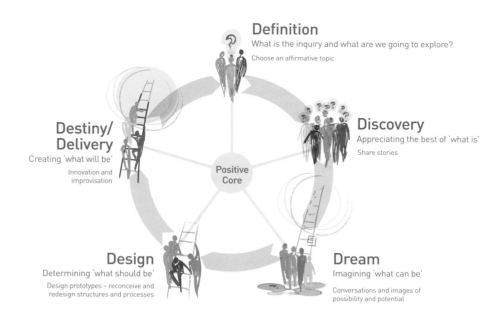

Mapping the 5Ds to the pastoral cycle

Working through the 5Ds is not a million miles from the well-trodden path, in Church circles, of the Pastoral cycle. Originating in the Young Catholic Workers movement under Cardinal Cardijn, who used the mantra see-judge-act, the Pastoral Cycle has been changed and adapted over the years, but has maintained that same sense of direction. The table below uses one of the simpler forms of the pastoral cycle, but shows how the different stages of the two methods of exploration correspond well to each other.[11]

Of course, the pastoral cycle is not a closed circle – we never end up in the same place. So the cycle is more of a loop in a pastoral cycle, which links to another key concept of Appreciative Inquiry – generativity. There will be further discussion of the pastoral cycle and the 5D cycle on the website: www.appreciating.church.

Pastoral Cycle *Let's do theology.* Laurie Green, Mowbray (1990)	**Appreciative Inquiry**
Experience : identifying the situation to be explored	**Definition**: choosing the topic and planning the approach
Exploration : finding out at much as possible	**Discovery**: sharing stories, hearing a variety of voices
Reflection : applying a faith perspective	**Dream**: imagining possibilities and potentials
Response : turning understanding into action	**Design**: redesigning the future
	Delivery: innovation and improvisation

Provocative propositions or future statements

The term 'provocative' is meant in the sense of being challenging and making people think. If the term 'provocative proposition' is too much of a challenge, a phrase like 'future statement' will often work.

"David Cooperrider (founder of AI) called the output of DESIGN 'provocative propositions' because he was trying to maximise generativity. Things that are provocative are, by definition, generative – they provoke/ generate thinking and action. A generative design phase will produce a house so beautiful, and so functional, people will be excited to build it and move in."

Gervase Bushe

---

11 With thanks to Kathryn Price for this mapping work.

Provocative propositions emerge from themes appearing in the dream stage and are developed in the design stage. They're uplifting statements about how an organisation, church, community or group goes forward, co-designs and co-creates its future.

Provocative propositions bridge the best of 'what is' with the ideas of 'what might be' (discovery and dream). They're provocative because they stretch the status quo – they can be uncomfortable, risky, edgy, challenge the way things have traditionally been done and offer new possibilities. A great provocative proposition can often name 'the elephant in the room' in an acceptable way.

Church examples

- The St Bride's provocative proposition is *Ensuring a safe sacred space for all*. This emerged through dialogue and co-creation.
- *"Whoever you are, wherever you are on life's journey, you are welcome here."* From United Churches of Christ (USA) campaign of radical welcome and adopted by a number of URC congregations.
- *"We are a welcoming, vibrant, loving community of followers of Jesus"*[12]
- *"Our living Lord meets us in worship – in word and sacrament, in praise and prayer – and that Sabbath encounter spills out into our daily lives"*[13]

Helpful hints:

- Remember, provocative propositions are one of the challenging parts of AI – it takes time and thought to create a good one. Paired conversations often help as a first stage in development;
- It's useful to start with 'we/I';
- Try and avoid long, all encompassing statements. Keep them short and exciting;
- Try and ensure they provoke thought, stretch, challenge, and push the status quo;
- Ensure they are grounded in the elements of the discovery and dream phase, and illustrate the ideal as a possibility;
- Do people want to do it? Does the congregation, organisation, community or group see it as their desired future and want to 'own it'?
- Is it generative? (see page 19) Does it have the 'wow' factor?
- Remember, it's not a mission statement!
- Foster passion and enthusiasm;
- Does it really challenge the congregation, organisation or community?
- Will it encourage adaptability, flexibility and innovation?
- Will it help create new working arrangements?
- Does it help to lead on to the delivery/destiny stage?
- Remember generativity and the AI principles.

"Be daring, be different, be impractical – be anything that will assert integrity of purpose and imaginative vision against the play-it-safers, the creatures of the commonplace, the slaves of the ordinary."

Sir Cecil Beaton

"Ask, and it will be given you;
search, and you will find;
knock, and the door will be opened for you." Matthew 7.7

---

12 Church of Scotland online book about AI, page 17 (see reading list)
13 as above...

SOAR™ (Strengths, Opportunities, Aspirations, Results/Resources)

"The task of leadership is to create an alignment of strengths, making our weaknesses irrelevant."

Peter Drucker

Created by Jackie Stavros and Gina Hinrichs (*The Thin Book of SOAR™: building strengths-based strategy*, 2009), SOAR™ is the Appreciative Inquiry contribution to strategic planning, and a generative alternative to a SWOT analysis. Moving from the dominant threats and weaknesses elements of SWOT, the SOAR™ approach encourages a more innovative and positive approach to strategic planning. Focusing on strengths and opportunities for individuals, churches and organisations is much more powerful and effective than dwelling on deficiencies. SOAR™ helps forward planning and development, generates enthusiasm and creates positive momentum. Weaknesses and threats are not ignored. They are reframed and given the appropriate focus within the opportunities and results conversations.

Practical examples of SOAR™ can be found in the *Resources* and *AI in Action* sections. As ever with AI, SOAR™ is a circular process – eg, the process of identifying strengths, opportunities, and aspirations, can lead to the discovery of additional opportunities.

SOAR™ approach	SWOT Analysis
Action orientated	Analysis orientated
Strengths and opportunities focus	Weaknesses and threats focus
Possibility focus	Competition focus
Innovation and breakthrough	Incremental improvement
Engagement of all levels	Top down → planning
Focus on implementation	Focus on analysis
Energy creating – We are good and can become great!	Energy depleting – there are so many weaknesses and threats!
Attention to results	Attention to gaps

(SOAR™ or SWOT comparison adapted from 'The Thin Book of SOAR™' – www.thinbook.com/pages/books/SOAR™_book.htm)

Strengths	**Opportunities**
Aspirations	**Resources/Results***

Helpful hints:

- Use an appreciative conversation to identify the strengths (page 31);
- SOAR™ works well within the design stage of the 5D cycle;
- Bring in generativity and AI principles at each stage;
- A useful question is 'what do we need to do differently'?
- For small business planning it can be very effective, and works well;
- Do not reject SWOT completely – it is sometimes useful, but in general it's just not as good as SOAR™;
- When using SOAR™ for personal development you can change 'results' to 'resources' – what people will need to move forward;
- Useful website: www.SOAR™-strategy.com.

"However beautiful the strategy, you should occasionally look at the results."

Winston Churchill

SOAR™ Development of the Spiritual SOAR™ exercise

This SOAR™ example describes how the AI tool SOAR™ was adapted to provide both a learning process and a practical exercise. Practical examples of SOAR™ can be found in the *Resources* and *AI in Action* sections. Notice how different it is from the traditional SWOT analysis.

Often the experience of designing and delivering an AI training workshop requires the creation of exercises and tasks that can help embed AI learning. These are normally done prior to the event but in this case it happened during the process. This is the story about the co-creation of the spiritual SOAR™ exercise.

It was developed at the first United Reformed Church *AI Basics* three-day course, run at the Windermere Centre in March 2014. Participants were made up of a mixture of Synod training officers, ministers and church related community workers. It was the final evening session of the second day, and the AI facilitators were about to introduce the SOAR™ tool and approach. Noticing a fall of energy in the room and a lack of focus at the end of a long day, the facilitators recognised the need to do something different. What was needed was a way of introducing the SOAR™ in a practical and interesting way. After a short ideas exchange, the table below was transcribed on to a flip chart and participants were asked to work in pairs to co-create their own personal spiritual SOAR™ journey plans.

The effect was fascinating and dramatic. There was a change in the energy, an increased conversation buzz and many continued working on them beyond the allotted time. Immediate feedback included comments like: 'It made me think; I found it a valuable personal learning, and a very practical way to learn about using a tool'. Post-course positive feedback continued with examples of successful use as part of Elders' meetings and as a personal spiritual development tool.

After a period of fine tuning the exercise was placed in the public library of the URC's learning environment. Feedback has continued to highlight its usefulness. Thought was given in the revision process to making the questions applicable to an audience beyond Christians. In autumn 2015, the exercise was shared with one of the internationally-linked AI groups. A number of users found it helpful, with positive comments from a young Muslim AI practitioner being a stand out response.

Our learning from the process was in two areas: the value of using practical experiences to help understand learning and the importance of providing accessible tools that people can easily use. The experience was a reminder of the importance and value of the simultaneity and poetic principles.

A SOAR™ for your spiritual journey

Strengths

What are the strengths in your day to day spiritual journey?

What do you value most in your spiritual life?

What are the most important parts of your spiritual life?

How does your spiritual practice support you in your daily life?

Opportunities

What opportunities are there for your spiritual life to grow?

How can you build on existing spiritual practice?

How you can utilise your spiritual life and practice more effectively?

Who can help to support you in your spiritual journey?

Aspirations

What are your dreams and hopes for your future spiritual life and journey?

What are the best ways for your spiritual practice to grow and expand?

What would a stronger and more supportive spiritual life look like for you?

How can your spiritual practice help you to feel freer?

Resources/Results*
(You can use either or both)

What resources do you need to help you in your spiritual journey?

Are there any additional connections to make that would help and support you?

What are the first two things you need to do next? (These can be simple steps and actions)

In what ways would you celebrate your learning and achievements?

How will you know that your spiritual life has grown and deepened?

Leaving the problems behind – helping people move away from a focus on problems

*"Though the fig tree does not blossom, and no fruit is on the vines;
though the produce of the olive fails and the fields yield no food;
though the flock is cut off from the fold and there is no herd in the stalls,
yet I will rejoice in the Lord;
I will exult in the God of my salvation."*

Habakkuk 3. 17-19

David Cooperrider explains why a problem-focused approach no longer serves organisations and groups:

• Problem-solving depresses groups and individuals;

• The cure is often worse than the disease;

• Problems can dominate and devalue the strengths and opportunities – an organisation that inquires into problems will keep finding problems;

• Problem-solving is driven primarily by a desire for relief rather than results.

Often, one of the challenges faced by people exploring and learning about Appreciative Inquiry is the struggle to move away from identifying problems and finding resolution. Here is a useful extract from a briefing on problem solving, much of which is drawn from Jane Magruder Watkins, Bernard Mohr and Ralph Kelly's book – *Appreciative Inquiry, Change at the speed of imagination.*

Dealing with negative comments. What about our problems?

- Traditional problem solving looks for what is wrong and 'fixes' it thereby returning the situation to the status quo.
- Appreciative Inquiry solves problems by seeking what is going right and building on it, thereby going beyond the original 'normal baseline'.

The term 'problem solving' carries a set of assumptions based on the paradigm that treats human systems like mechanical ones. We have all been taught to solve problems in human systems based on the following assumptions:

- There is some ideal way for things to be;
- If a situation is not as we would like it to be, it is a 'problem' to be solved;
- The way to solve a problem is to break it into parts and analyse it;
- If we find a broken part and fix it, the whole will be fixed.

The process for solving problems in the current paradigm follows:

- Identifying what's wrong;
- Analysing the causes;
- Deciding on goals to fix these causes;
- Making a plan that will achieve the goals;
- Implementing the plan;
- Evaluating whether we fixed the problem or not.

Having embraced the concept of the socially constructed reality, we can look at the same problems from the AI perspective based on these assumptions:

- *'The way things are'* is socially constructed by our system and therefore can be changed;
- In any situation, we can find the seeds of excellence to build on;
- We build on excellence by seeking out examples and sharing stories throughout the system;
- As we create images of excellence, our system will move toward that image.

The process of solving *'problems'* in the emerging paradigm follows:

- Let's look at our experience in the area that we want to improve in order to discover the times when things were going well – times when we felt excited successful, joyful;
- From these stories we can collectively create a description for what we're seeking (our image of the ideal);
- We can go out and ask others how they have successfully dealt with a similar situation;
- We can share our images; discover the images that others hold. And continually re-create a generative and creative future throughout the system.

Moving from the problem solving approach takes time and practice. The Centre of Learning from Excellence in Birmingham (learningfromexcellence.com/) has developed a user friendly process for 'Reporting on Excellence'. It includes a good summary of advice for facilitators and interviewers on dealing with the negatives.

What to do with negatives

The aim of this process is learning from positives, but people should not feel like they do not have permission to also talk about things that need fixing.

There are several different ways to handle negatives.

- **Postponing:** Say that you would like to make a note of what the person has said and come back to it later. When you get to the question about what he or she would wish for the organisation in the future, this is the time to discuss the 'negative' data.

- **Listening:** If the person has some real intensity about problems, let him or her express it. If it is the major focus of the person's energy, you are not going to get any positive data until she or he gets it out. This may mean muddling through quite a bit of organisational negativity, and the biggest threat is that you will take it in and lose your capacity to be appreciative. Keep a caring, and affirmative spirit.

- **Redirecting:** If the person is adamant about dealing with the negative, or if you have listened sufficiently to understand the negative issues being raised, find a way to guide the person back to the positive: "I think I understand a little bit about some of the problems you see (paraphrase a few of the ones you've heard), and now I would like to guide us back to looking at what is happening when things are working at their best.

- **Using negative data:** Everything that people find wrong with an organisation represents an absence of something that they hold in their minds as an ideal. For example, if the interviewee says something like, 'The communication in this organisation is terrible', say to them, 'When you say that the communication is terrible, it means that you have some image in your mind about what good communication would look like. Can you describe that for me?' In fact, one could argue that there is no such thing as negative data. Use the negative information and reframe it into a wish or vision statement and then confirm that statement with the interviewee.

Source: learningfromexcellence.com/

Contribution of positive psychology and positive emotions to AI

"Appreciative Inquiry is the first cousin of Positive Psychology"
Professor Martin Seligman – one of the founders of positive psychology

Appreciative Inquiry research and effectiveness has increasingly drawn from the field of positive psychology, which is the scientific study of positive aspects of human life, such as happiness, wellbeing and flourishing. Positive psychology looks at how these qualities develop and grow and how can we maintain them. Professor Martin Seligman believes that a happier society requires us to pay more attention to the quality of our inner life, and to use proven methods to improve it.

That is what positive psychology is about – the exercises and approach it offers include the systematic practice of kindness, gratitude to others, counting your blessings and exploiting your strengths rather than attacking your weaknesses. It also teaches resilience and optimism. It is the key component to ensuring wellbeing.

By contrast, the fruit of the Spirit is love, joy, peace, patience, kindness, generosity, faithfulness, gentleness and self-control. There is no law against such things.
Galatians 5.22-23

Some positive psychology research findings:

- People are generally happy;
- Money does not necessarily buy wellbeing: but spending money on other people does;
- Some of the best ways to combat disappointments and setbacks include social relationships and character strengths;
- Work can be important to wellbeing, especially when people are able to engage in work that is purposeful and meaningful;
- While happiness is influenced by genetics, people can learn to be happier by developing optimism, gratitude and altruism.

"Our congregation is small and elderly, with one or two young people. One of them did badly in his exams but spoke of how much he enjoyed being part of the church because we encouraged and supported him and didn't hold his results against him."
Church member

Dr Barbara Fredrickson, author of *Positivity and Love 2.0*, is a leading scholar in the area of positive psychology. Her 'broaden-and-build' theory explains why positive emotions change your perspective on life and how they can help you develop valuable emotional resources, such as resilience and mindfulness. She has found, in over 20 years of research, that individuals need to keep a certain ratio of positive emotions to negative ones in order to flourish. The video *Positive Emotions Open Our Mind* highlights her work – you can watch it on YouTube.

Three particularly notable things about positive emotions are:

- They help us to be more open. For example, a number of experiments have been done where giving students a gift of sweets before an exam helps them feel more positive before they start and they then do better in the exam;
- They help people find better 'win-win' solutions;
- They help people to be more resilient.

"So let us not grow weary in doing what is right, for we will reap at harvest-time, if we do not give up. So then, whenever we have an opportunity, let us work for the good of all, and especially for those of the family of faith."
Galatians 6.9-10

AI in action.
Stories and
experiences from
a wide range of
church settings

PART TWO:

AI in action. Stories and experiences from a wide range of church settings

These are further stories and experiences of AI at work from the denominations involved in the *Appreciating Church* project. Contributors have shared the tools, tasks, and questions they used, as well as their experiences and the learning they gained. Some describe using the major tools such as the 5D process, the AI protocols and SOAR™, whilst others are about a small piece of AI where just a few questions or a single paired conversation has been included in existing organisational arrangements.

The stories are written from authentic experience and carry the voice and texture of the storytellers. The formats vary from descriptions of process development to case studies and interview transcripts. In some cases, the original formatting of material has been retained for the sake of clarity. We have included as much practical advice and information as possible as resources which you can use and adapt. As more examples emerge from other church and community processes they will be included in the website: www.appreciating.church.

Each example is introduced by a note about context, observations, and potential learning to be gained.

In these two short case studies, Fiona Thomas of the United Reformed Church describes how a paired conversation within a departmental meeting can contribute to building relationships. In the second case study the AI process provides space for the group to identify and build on success.

❶ United Reformed Church Discipleship Department

The first meeting of the Discipleship Department at the URC in its new form

The purpose of the gathering was for people to get to know each other, share ideas about their work, and be updated on *Walking the Way*, a major new emphasis in the life of the URC. There was a lot to cover in a relatively short time. Of the 16 members of staff of the department, 12 were present at the meeting. After coffee and cake, people were invited to move into 20 minute paired conversations with someone they wanted to get to know better, asking two questions:

Q1 What's been the best piece of work that you've done with someone outside your particular part of the URC? What makes it stand out for you?

Q2 What are your strengths? (Name up to three).

The pairs then joined together in fours, and were asked to:

a. share the highlights of their conversation, listing their strengths on Post-its;

b. identify the questions they had about *Walking the Way. Living the Life of Jesus Today.*

This was generative: people were able to identify strengths and when those strengths were pooled via Post-it notes, it became clear this was a very resourceful group of people:

Unflappable	Opening up	Relationship building
Administration (behind the scenes)	Advocacy	Organised
Seeing the big picture clearly	Sense of humour	Analytical
IT and technology	Patience	Positive and optimistic
Sociable and approachable	Commitment	Imagination
Team enabling	Persistence	Loyalty
Bringing people together	Listening	Resilience
Team playing	Spontaneous	Creativity
Encourager	Empathy	Children's work locally
	Public speaking	Experiences
	Good listener	
	Diplomacy/Tact	
	Enthusiasm	

The next discussion was on how best to work together, especially on the shared programme of *Walking the Way*. The rest of the morning was shared between updating people on the programme's intention and looking at the floor plans for refurbishment of the building. The latter would require the whole of the staff to move to temporary premises for six months.

Observations

The listeners were careful not to jump in with their own stories but to focus on the questions being asked. It's not often that people get asked to name their strengths. When people share their strengths together, this generates a joyful recognition that the group is a strong resource. It was a good exercise in engagement: no doubt the coffee and cake helped.

Within the Discipleship Department many people are already used to working in flexible ways. The result of this AI exercise was to encourage and engage people collaboratively.

Impact

When the team leaders met afterwards, they responded positively to the meeting, feeling that it had been well facilitated. Fiona recorded the results from the morning meeting and emailed them to everyone afterwards with the expectation of building on this foundation in subsequent departmental meetings.

> One of the realities to wrestle with is that although we are a department, we still operate in separate teams. Nonetheless, a step has been taken forward: in future we might ask questions about the scope of the work we are doing so we arrive at a common task together and integrate our work, rather than everyone staying in their own corners, telling each other about their work but not necessarily doing the work together, which has been the inherited pattern. Appreciative Inquiry could help us become a more integrated department if we use it consistently and intentionally.
>
> Fiona Thomas, reflecting afterwards

❷ Christian Aid workshop, facilitated by Fiona Thomas

I was invited by the Forest Group of United Reformed Church congregations in East London to the annual weekend marking the anniversary of its formation, which in 2016 coincided with the end of Christian Aid Week.

Saturday workshop

The purpose of the day was to learn more about Christian Aid, working from the assumption that people had been involved with the organisation for some time. The day started with a reflection on Psalm 90 verse 10, which speaks of people living for three score years and ten, and picking up on the 70 years of existence which Christian Aid had marked the previous year.

I then showed a series of films which spanned the decades of Christian Aid's work and, after each short film, asked people to reflect on what they'd seen with the person sitting next to them. People were struck by how society had changed over the decades, and encouraged by their own positive experiences of Christian Aid. They were surprised by what they *hadn't* known – for instance the response of Christian Aid in the aftermath of World War II to refugees from Europe and how this related to today; and also how these films showed the dramatic change in how the church is viewed by society.

I asked people to form pairs for an appreciative conversation about Christian Aid Week around the following questions, given to them as a handout with space to keep notes:

Questions:

1. Tell me a story of when you have been glad to be part of Christian Aid Week.
2. What's the best aspect of the Forest Group of Churches involvement in Christian Aid?
3. What do you think needs to be done differently to make Christian Aid Week even more effective in the Forest Group?
4. What's the smallest step and the most radical step you could take to deepen the Forest Group's involvement with Christian Aid?

The pairs were brought together in fours and I asked the groups to identify their five actions for making the Forest Group's involvement with Christian Aid even more effective.

Dream phase

I asked people to imagine, in two years' time, the director of Christian Aid coming to thank the Forest Group for the substantial amount of money they had raised. They were to imagine how they might have raised that money. This prompted people to think about what they were good at, and identify the strengths of each church. Working as if it had all happened, people produced posters of the concerts they had performed, the cake stalls they had run, and the various new ways of fundraising that they had devised. They worked in mixed groups during this exercise, learning from each other. This helped cohesion across the churches and to cement understanding of each other.

People went away from the day saying: 'we know how to do it now!' They had come up with ideas that were practical and possible, so they had moved into design. This was one step further forward into their discomfort zone than they had imagined, but they saw how it was possible.

The session concluded with a valuation exercise in which I asked participants to write the answers to three short questions on separate Post-its. I later typed these up and sent them to the group leaders:

- What was good about today?
- What did I learn?
- What am I going to do?

Good about today answers included:

- Planning things together;
- meeting other church members;
- fellowship;
- bringing people together;
- mixing with other members of Forest Churches;
- companionship; humour; getting together;
- working together;
- raising money to Christian Aid;
- seeing how money raised is used;
- sharing ideas;
- fellowship with Forest Group;
- sharing ideas;
- fellowship of group;
- working together and dreaming;
- a mixture of observation and participation;
- learning and working together;
- working together with members of the Forest Group of different venues and ages;
- learning about Christian Aid history;
- group activities showed different viewpoints; sharing ideas.

Participants learned about:

- The abilities of others and their skills;
- more about Christian Aid;
- the story of Christian Aid;
- more info about Christian Aid;
- it is good to be united;
- working together;
- how Christian Aid has developed over 70 years;
- the churches would be able to accomplish more together;
- history of Christian Aid;
- joint forces give lots of good energy;
- ideas for the future;
- many heads – many ideas;
- age of Christian Aid as a charity;
- origin of Christian Aid;
- the work of Christian Aid in the last 70 years;
- interested to hear that Christian Aid developed from refugee crisis of 1945 – relevant to same today?;
- others' experiences;
- we can do more together;
- amount of talent;
- Christian Aid work in Bangladesh;
- the length of time Christian Aid has been going (not quite as long as myself);
- more about Christian Aid Week.

Participants planned to:

- Pray;
- get more involved;
- be more pro-active;
- help to ensure some of our ideas come to fruition;
- make our fund-raising concert a success;
- get together more!; encourage the success of aims;
- put into practice what I learned today;
- ask Questers if they would like to do the *Church Walk the City* if it's on in 2017;
- plan for 2018;
- organise book sale for Christian Aid;
- commitment for the future;
- take ideas back to our church; find out the bank of resources and talents the Forest Group contains;
- support our work with Forest Group;
- keep on promoting Group aim(s);
- working together;
- think of one Forest-wide Forest-inclusive event before I go;
- helping all those in trouble;
- do what I can to help;
- to try to work along with others in the Forest Group to support Christian Aid;
- try to be more pro-active, work with other people and church;
- need fundraising events;
- ask my sisters what they would do for Christian Aid.

Outcomes

Four months later it was reported to me by one of the ministers in the Forest Group that people had remembered their dreams and were encouraging each other to implement the actions that they'd identified.

Facilitator's reflection on both examples

The paired conversations gave people a chance to bring their own stories to the surface and it is really valuable to do the valuation exercise. It's about intentionality, trusting the process and finding the way of using AI in everything that I do. It is possible to use it even in small ways. Each time I use it, it makes a difference.

❸ AI supporting development of Quaker eldership and oversight

This Quaker example demonstrates how the AI 5D process can support people to move away from a deficit-based, problem-solving focus. Note how the impact and effectiveness of the approach continues after the initial event.

Zélie Gross

Through the experience of using AI with Friends in recent years, I've seen the potential for how this approach can support the work we do to put our faith into action – in our communities and in our outward witness. Quakers can be as prone as any group to seeing issues as problems to be solved, but we do live with an understanding of 'that of God' in everyone. It's a guiding principle in how we approach relationships with people and how we respond to challenging situations. In other words, we seek to recognise the positive and we aspire to build on whatever is hopeful.

When one of my aims for an event is to help Friends understand Appreciative Inquiry and how to work with it, I explicitly use a 5D process, or parts of the cycle, and describe each stage in those terms. More often, I integrate AI principles and processes into events or courses as the best way I know of generating lively engagement in a group and a positive atmosphere. When a small task group signals to me to leave them alone – please – because they are so engrossed, I know it's working.

A sequence of session titles for a typical single day event designed to explore ways of developing eldership and oversight practice with a local or area meeting might look like this:

1. The building blocks of eldership and oversight;
2. Our meeting(s) – what are we already doing well?
3. Aspects of our practice we aspire to build on;
4. Firming up intentions;
5. Making things happen.

There's no mention here of AI, and I don't explain it in those terms on the day, but the programme reveals the 5Ds at work:

- Session one defines our area of enquiry, as agreed, and we use this session to revisit our understanding of eldership and oversight as a whole group, and then through paired conversations to identify aspects of particular interest to this group on this occasion.

- Session two opens up discovery of gifts and strengths among the Friends present and in their meeting(s) – a joyful process of conversations and whole-group sharing that invariably leaves Friends feeling thoroughly good about themselves. Bearing in mind that elders, overseers and others can easily fell despondent about the realities and demands of eldership and oversight, it's a great achievement and a great springboard for the rest of the day.

- I then invite Friends to 'dream', to imagine how they can have more of the good things they've discovered about themselves, their meeting, their eldership and oversight practice. This is when I introduce visual and creative ways of exploring our theme; I encourage play and use of metaphor.

- Moving on, we focus on how we articulate our intentions; we 'design' how changes and developments we've imagined as possibilities can actually work within the wider structure of a meeting.

- That's often enough for one day, but I hope not to end until we've at least opened up the question of what happens next, how intentions will be 'delivered'. This is a big question, which an event of this kind may not be able to answer, as it typically rests with further discernment in each local meeting. But here we clarify the processes Friends will be working with and the range of tasks ahead. We may close with agreeing a 'minute', expressing 'the sense' of this gathering, to be brought to a local or area meeting for worship for business.

The 5D process described here naturally – and intentionally – incorporates the core principles of AI in each stage, while my overriding aim as facilitator is to keep the progress of the day 'generative'. Are we coming up with ideas that move us on? Are our perceptions and previous assumptions changing such that there's no going back? Are we surprising ourselves with the value and potential of the new things emerging?

As an external facilitator, I can't always assess the lasting effects of events I run on the life of meetings, but I do keep bumping into Friends who tell me how very useful they found an event, how they were changed personally and the differences they see in their meeting. I find that encouraging, and evidence enough that AI can help Quakers further their vision for the Society.

❹ The Methodist Church: developing the Discipleship and Ministries Learning Network

Richard Armiger from the Methodist Church demonstrates how an AI activity can be built into a wider event. This example shows the early part of the 5D cycle combined with a useful and effective appreciative evaluation process.

Learning and development across the Connexion (The Methodist Church in Britain) is supported by the Discipleship and Ministries Learning Network (DMLN), which was established in September 2013. This work has four aims:

* nurturing and equipping Christ-like disciples;
* challenging and equipping mission-shaped communities;
* forming and equipping those who share in lay and ordained ministry;
* enabling and encouraging creative thinkers in an environment of scholarship, research and innovation.

The DMLN functions as:

* 11 teams located in regions
* three teams focusing on a particular specialism: discipleship development; church and community development; ministry development
* two centres: Cliff College, Derbyshire and The Queen's Foundation, Birmingham

The DMLN gathers twice a year as a whole staff team at Cliff College in Derbyshire, which also offers the opportunity for staff to gather in their specialist groups to develop the work in the relevant specialist area.

At the DMLN Gathering in May 2016 the focus was on one of the four DMLN priorities: 'Healthy Methodist Communities'. In particular we were looking at how the network might continue to grow and flourish as a community. We were also using the gathering to give an initial introduction to Appreciative Inquiry (AI) to the whole DMLN team as we seek to develop its use within our work and practice. There is a recognition that AI provides a way of focusing on what is life-giving and generative in any given context, enabling these things to 'appreciate' or 'increase' in value.

We used elements of AI in each of the specialist team sessions. The following example is based on the AI approach for the discipleship development specialists' session. In order to work through the 'Definition' stage and to establish the inquiry, the facilitator met with the Discipleship Development Coordinator and the Discipleship Development Officer who are based at Cliff College. Following the conversation the topic of 'being called' was decided for the inquiry. 'Being called' is part of 'a strategy framework for discipleship development' within the Methodist Church. In this context we were looking at one aspect within that of 'experiencing and exploring faith at an introductory level'. The purpose of the inquiry was to explore how this aspect of discipleship development might be taken forward through the DMLN within the Methodist Church.

The session at the gathering was initially allocated three hours, in two 90-minute sessions. The elements of the 5D process that we used at the gathering were discovery, dream and design, with delivery followed up within the team after the gathering. The intention was to use AI principles to develop this aspect of the work through a generative approach and enable it to flourish. By using the AI principles in this way we were also familiarising the learning and development staff within the DMLN with AI through an experiential learning approach.

The aim was to reach the point of generating a number of different ways in which this aspect of the work could be taken forward through the discipleship development specialists.

This outline was produced as a guide for facilitating the session, with handouts given of some of the material.

Flourishing – 'being called'

Discovery (90 minutes in total)

In pairs, reflect on your initial sense of being called as a disciple:

Paired conversation (30 minutes)

1. Share the story of your own sense of being called into a relationship with God/ when you made a commitment to follow God. Who else was involved? How did you feel?
2. What surprised and excited you the most about being called?
3. Who provided support to you at that time? What form did that support take?
4. Reflecting on your on ongoing relationship with God what are the things that sustain you and encourage you?

In your pairs, one person answers the questions while the other listens. As you listen use the space below (and overleaf) to record the key words, phrases and story elements that come from what is being shared. The person listening may help support the conversation and go deeper by asking supplementary questions such as: Tell me more? Who else was involved? What were you thinking? How were you feeling?

After 15 minutes, swap roles for a further 15 minutes.

Key words, phrases and story elements:

Join with another pair to form a group of four (30 minutes)

Take it in turns to briefly share each other's stories – with the one who listened sharing the story of the other. Highlight the key words or phrases that were noted. (10 minutes)

Identify common insights or phrases i.e. patterns repeated in varied experience. Use the flip chart paper to capture these reflections. (10 minutes)

Reflect together on the following points (10 minutes):

* Where are the places that you see people being called to faith today within the Methodist Church?
* What is it about these places that enable people to be called to faith?
* As a group identify up to seven key elements that enable people to hear and respond to God's call, and express these in short phrases.

As a whole group (20 minutes)

Present back each of the group flip charts.

Dream (60 minutes in total)

In your group of four:

It's May 2018 and we are meeting as a team to celebrate the successful discipleship programme and in particular the impact it is making in relation to 'being called'.

Looking back to May 2016, explain what you did. What are the challenges that you faced and how did you address them? What helped to take you forward? What does 'being called' look and feel like when it is flourishing?

Please share the journey, the impact and the successes on the way, including the challenges overcome.

* Reflect individually on your response (5 minutes)
* Share your individual response with your group and discuss (40 minutes)

Find a way of expressing what 'being called' looks like when it's flourishing – in whatever medium you want, whether this is a poem, song, play, flip chart or something else and prepare to present it to everyone.

As a whole group (15 minutes):

a)   What have you noticed from all that has been presented?

b)   What things excite you, from what has been identified?

c)   Where is God in all of this?

Design (15 minutes)

What steps can we take to enable this work to flourish?

	Me	Us (who)	Others (who)
Now			
Next			
Eventually			

In each box, identify one small thing and one big thing that would enable this aspect of discipleship development to flourish

Feedback from the AI activity

1. **What did you enjoy about the process?**

   - Conversation based
   - Telling / listening to stories
   - 'Being' together
   - The opportunity to share in detail with others
   - Sharing in pairs our stories of 'being called'
   - Engaging with an important topic
   - Some form of structure
   - Ability to share deeply with colleagues

2. **What did you learn from the approach?**

   - Need longer for each element
   - All need to understand the process
   - Positive focus
   - More about others
   - Finding points of connection
   - The value of recognising, valuing and seeking to build on the diversity of the experience and perspective in the group
   - We as a team are all actively engaged in helping people engage with God. We have changed, not other people. Helping people recognise that God is already at work in our life.
   - Similarities in our understanding of 'being called'
   - Being called 'a journey'
   - Keep this conversation going until we get an outcome

3. **What did you value about the conversations and tasks?**

   - The honesty. The deep listening and sharing
   - The buzz, honesty, diversity
   - Tasks were clear and limited
   - Enjoyed getting to hear someone's story
   - A clear structure
   - Being challenged to think outside of the box
   - Growing the conversation outwards

4. **What is the first step you are going to do to move discipleship development forward?**

   - I'm going to keep it up in the region, as in this place we never get anywhere
   - Talk to more people in my network about their views on 'being called' and 'discipleship'

Running the session

The session itself ended up needing to be shortened, which meant that we only had one hour for the second part. That led to a change in the approach as the session was running. Whilst this worked well enough, one reflection was that time is needed in order to work through each of the 5Ds, so it's vital to allocate sufficient time, as far as possible.

Allocating an hour and a half for the discovery stage recognised that this would allow the members of the discipleship development team to spend time getting to know one another at a deeper level through the protocols that were devised for this stage. This produced additional benefits and impact above and beyond the initial scope of the process. Some of the feedback that was received after the process, in terms of what people enjoyed, learned and valued about the process, highlighted this through phrases such as:

- The value of recognising, valuing and seeking to build on the diversity of the experience and perspective in the group
- 'Being' together
- Ability to share deeply with colleagues
- The honesty. The deep listening and sharing

Overall, the approach that we took worked well and enabled the group to move forward as a whole, both in response to the specific area of work and also as a team. One positive difference for subsequent use would be to have sufficient time for each of the individual elements within the process. However, having time limits on the various stages was important and the feedback showed that it was valued by those participating.

❺ Helping a congregation to move forward

This AI story is provided by Kathryn Price from the United Reformed Church to demonstrate an experience of using AI at a challenging point in the life of a congregation.

The context and process

The church was just beginning to emerge from the mourning period following the retirement of their minister, who had been with them for 15 years. Although I was the congregation's Interim Moderator[1], it was as the Synod Education and Learning Enabler that I was invited to help the congregation begin to relearn who they were without the Minister at the helm and to explore their vision for the future.

So, on the first Sunday in Lent, I led worship on the theme, *Faith, joy, hope and love in the wilderness*. After coffee we went into the hall, set up with tables and a shared lunch.

---

1 A voluntary transitional position in the United Reformed Church deployed during a ministerial vacancy to support the congregation.

Encouragingly, most of the congregation joined in. You can see our timetable for the afternoon, with the process pattern in this box:

This is our story – this is our song

12 noon   Introduction – interim ministry process
- What is an active pastorate profile?
- How church meeting works at its best

Where are we being called? What is our vision? Can we identify priorities for mission and ministry?

Principles – listen, be honest, don't gossip

12.15   First conversation – what has been a high point in your membership here?
- Why was that so?
- First in twos, then fours, then plenary

12.45   Lunch and during lunch:
- Second conversation – what is this church good at? (Give a real example)
- In small groups

1.30   - List of high points – are there still such possibilities?
- List of what the church is good at – how might it be better?

2.00   Third 'conversation'
- *For the sake of the Gospel, I would like this church to be known as the church that . . .*
- Individual Post-it notes
- Put dreams up in groups, i.e. like with like

2.20   Priorities
- Give everyone six sticky spots. Put stickers against your choices (spread three, two, one – or all in one place)

2.45   What happens next?
- All the results will be written into a report, published in the church magazine
- Elders will look at the priorities and identify what steps might be needed to achieve them.

The initial outcome

Afterwards, as promised, all the notes were written up for the elders to discuss, and from them came a new mission statement for the church and some new priorities, some of which were taken up straightaway. An article was written for the church magazine, so that everyone was kept up to date with progress (see *This is our story, this is our song* overleaf).

What made it work well? The introduction through the Sunday morning worship helped. Sitting around tables over a meal was another factor, but also the fact that people were asked to speak for themselves and use their own experiences. Talking – sometimes in twos or fours, and sometimes in larger groups – and also thinking individually, broke the session up and kept the mood lively.

I have also used this process with a group of elders on an away day. There the thinking was perhaps deeper and more focused and intentional, but the 'three conversations' will work in a variety of settings.

This is our story, this is our song

Three questions, leading to three conversations over lunch:

* what has been a high point in your time at the URC and what made it so?
* what is the URC good at and can you provide evidence?
* how would you finish the following sentence? *For the sake of the Gospel, I would want the URC to be known as 'the church that...'*

Because there was a range of people gathered around the lunch tables, there was a range of answers:

High points included friendship, worship, outreach, special personal days, Easter mornings. The outward-looking nature of the church was important to some, as was the reform discussion group and the generosity of the congregation. These things were valued because of the welcome, inclusive, supportive atmosphere and the willingness of folk to get on and do things, especially after *[named minister]* retired. The depth of thought, both theological and social action focused, was also appreciated.

So what are we good at? Well – caring was high on the list, whether that be caring for each other and particularly lonely isolated members or for those in need, both here and abroad. There was plenty of evidence for this – Oasis, food bank volunteers, the setting up of Work-Wise and the practical side of pastoral care (offering lifts, for example). Worship, welcome and eating together were more of our strengths, with people coming back after an initial visit. Working with others was also in evidence, with the Christmas Tree Festival cited as a prime example. We take good care of our buildings too.

As for that last question, there were as many answers as people at lunch. More in fact, as some had more than one response. The full list will go on the notice board, but the answers could be usefully grouped this way:

— is welcoming and caring;
— has a concern for social justice;
— likes to learn;
— is a spiritual place;
— works ecumenically;
— reaches out to others;
— plays its part in the life of the town.

Of course there were concerns expressed:

* how can we sustain our church life, when we are all growing older?
* how can we let other people know about us and find out what they think too?

However, we were reminded that we are only called to be faithful, to be the church we can be at our best and that means being realistic, but hopeful, in our vision.

So what happens now?

The elders will look at the full results and begin to formulate a new vision to bring to the church meeting, from which priorities for action will drawn up. Everyone's thoughts are important, so if you were not able to be at the lunch, let an elder know what your answers would have been and join in the conversation.

Kathryn Price

❻ Highway Hope and the New Covenant Church. Using AI to support a community plan

This is an Appreciating People-facilitated project, part of the First Steps programme, to help a church community devise a local plan.

The New Covenant Church in Levenshulme, Manchester, is part of 50 UK African Pentecostal Churches with roots in Nigeria. Established in 2001, it has grown into a significant worshipping community with a local community purpose of supporting the most disadvantaged. As well as a Saturday School the converted ex-Job Centre hosts and supports a range of community services including café, clothes shop and second hand furniture retail outlet, and unemployment support services.

These services are provided through the church's charitable arm Highway Hope, founded in 2012. The charity's aims are to improve the lives of local residents of Manchester (especially Levenshulme, Longsight and Gorton), and especially those who are isolated and vulnerable, with a vision to transform lives, and empower and support local residents within the community. Its mission is to improve the health and wellbeing of the community through a range of multi-purpose cultural, social and learning activities. Levenshulme is one of the poorest districts in Greater Manchester.

In 2015 Highway Hope received a grant under the Department for Communities and Local Government (DCLG) *First Steps* programme, to support the creation of a Local Community Action plan. The project included additional support from a relationship manager to provide advice, guidance and training. Appreciating People was asked to take on this role.

> In our charity, we see that people in our community have been struggling and we wanted to help them. We acknowledge that the people who use our charity are very strong as they are survivors from many of life's tough challenges and we hope to build their self-esteem. Many have come through and survived huge disadvantage and barriers.
>
> We came up with the aim of our charity to be one of encouraging people. We want to see people thrive and flourish. 'Flourishing and Nourishing'. The focus of our charity therefore is a plan for overall health and well being, including physical and mental health.
>
> We looked at one person who uses the centre and analysed how we have captured her story, out of the complexity and chaos of her life. This gave us the idea about how we would like to give others the opportunity to tell their story through the First Step's programme.
>
> *Excerpt from the Highway Hope community plan*

Approach/ methodology

At an early stage of the planning process, it became clear that the traditional engagement model of community surveys and public events would not include 'all the voices' and many of the people Highway Hope wanted to connect with would not take part in these types of arrangements. These early discussions also highlighted significant literacy issues which would diminish the value of community surveys.

With the support of Appreciating People, the planning group co-designed a five stage process based on the use of AI. This used a combination of paired and group conversations with community users of the centre and its services, and the wider worshipping community. The worshipping community are essential Highway Hope stakeholders, taking part in a range of community activities and providing both financial and personnel support. The process including the training and design stages ran for five months and engaged over 300 people.

Five stage process:

1. Small project group agreed questions and identified target individuals
2. Appreciative Conversation training for small group of conversation interviewers plus question testing
3. Conversations took place with community users and the wider church community
4. Design workshop considered all the emerging themes from the conversations, and fed them into the emerging plan
5. The 'generativity' from the process was experienced in the church's large group session, with new ideas and clear support for the Highway Hope work.

Planning group and appreciative conversation training

The first stage was the formation of a planning group drawn from the staff and community volunteers. This small group received appreciative conversation skills training and co-created the conversation questions and how the process was delivered.

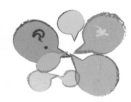

Community conversations

From October 2015 to February 2016, Highway Hope users and participants took part in myriad conversations. These conversations were based on the following appreciative conversation protocol. Examples of responses are given in bold italics:

Q1 *Think of a time or experience when your involvement and engagement with Highway to Hope has made a difference to you. Share it as a story.*

   "Highway Hope supports me with the food bank and also with work experience"

Q2 *How does Highway Hope support and help you. It can be the smallest thing.*

   "Providing shoulders to cry on"

Q3 *What is special about this place and the people involved?*

   "Helping shape the community"; "Being there for everyone"

Q4 *In your experience what does this place and its community do really well?*

   "Highway Hope supplied me with food bank support programme at time of need"

Q5 *What do you think needs to be done differently to make this community even better?*

   "More groups working together"; "Better equipment for all departments"

Q6 *What would be the things or activities that could help you even more? Share a simple step*

   "Improve my chances to get a job"; "Have simple steps to help organise activities to reach out to wider community"

Church community conversations

In November 2015, at the end of the Sunday worship, community conversations took place with 300 people from the teenage church and the adult church. Both groups were asked three questions and were facilitated by the conversation-trained interviewers. The questions were:

Q1 How does Highway Hope help this church?

Q2 What is important about the work of Highway Hope?

Q3 What does Highway Hope need to do differently?

Following this conversation, the participants were asked to complete Post-it notes identifying any key points and ideas. The Teenage Church conducted their session slightly differently by combining feedback by Post-it notes and group flip charts.

Examples of the responses in the church session included:

- "Helps the community develop different skills"
- "Highway Hope has helped the church make Christianity practical – feed the hungry, clothe the naked"
- "Platform for interaction between people"
- "It treats all races the same and has some diversity"
- "Gives people a place to feel comfortable and express themselves"
- "It has respect in the local community by bringing in the local people and attending to the needs of the people both spiritually and materially."

Planning group and next steps

The remaining stages of identifying the emergent themes from the conversations and co-designing the community plan were completed by the planning group.

Alongside providing content for the community action plan, the process recognised that:

- Participants face multiple challenges in living in a vicious circle of mental ill-health, lack of skills and knowledge, lack of self-confidence and just surviving on a day to day basis;
- The worshipping community both celebrated and supported the impact Highway Hope had on the local community;
- There are limitations in the existing resources and premises and a need for the charity to expand provision to meet increased demand.

Since the plan has been submitted, the church has improved the facilities and is now identifying ways to increase provision and find larger premises.

The focus of this project from Highway Hope was to create a community plan. AI questions and protocols were the core element of this. From an AI perspective, the learning was in four areas:

1. The value in training local people to ask the appreciative questions and also to co-create the questions supported by a small project group;
2. Just using a range of appreciative conversations was sufficient to gather the required information;
3. Using a flexible model of combining paired and small group conversations engaged people with the process who would not normally take part in the traditional community engagement processes;
4. The process encouraged all the voices to be heard.

❼ St Bride's: Appreciative Inquiry-based model for a church plan

This is another Appreciating People-facilitated project.

> The St Bride's process provides a practical example of a church going through elements of the AI 5D process.This is one way of approaching a church plan and each instance will be shaped by its particular context. It is interesting to note:
>
> a. how the AI process supported the church when facing the crisis over the future of their building;
>
> b. good examples of AI provocative propositions emerging in stage four;
>
> c. how the richness of the interview content led to the creation of poems and liturgies as can be seen in the worship resources section.
>
> For examples of the AI questions and tasks developed by St Bride's, see the resources section page 86.

The St Bride's AI experience provides a framework for creating an AI plan based on the 5D process described in Part Two of *Appreciating Church*. This story focuses on appreciative conversations, a series of church community events, and the impact of the process, including how the church faced a major unanticipated financial challenge with its building.

You can find St Bride's conversation protocols and guidance in the resources section on page 86.

Context

St Bride's Anglican Church in Toxteth, an inner city suburb in the Diocese of Liverpool, had a congregation of five when Rev Guy Elsmore arrived as Rector in 2005. He was tasked with the charge to 'do something different or close it.' It now attracts up to 100 worshippers during some Sundays, with a diverse range of liturgies.[2]

St Bride's opened in 1831 in the city's Georgian Quarter, then a wealthy part of the city. Extensive demolition of houses in the early 1970s ripped the heart out of the area and the church's congregation plummeted.

Faced with the challenge of how to ensure the church's survival, Guy and his colleagues began discussions with local residents on how to revitalise the building, which is close to the city centre and two of its universities. The vision statement they co-created to relaunch the parish in 2007 was:

> **St Bride's is a community with a radical vision of faith and a great history**
>
> In listening to our faith and the needs of the parish we serve, three themes have emerged strongly:
>
> • **A CREATIVE church**: A place where people, the visual arts, music and faith mix together.
>
> • **A PROGRESSIVE church**: A place where the Christian story is lived and explored in a way that respects questions as much as answers with an openness to the insights of science and the ways of other faiths.
>
> • **An INCLUSIVE church**: A place where everyone can feel respected and at home, regardless of sexuality, gender, race, disability, class or creed.

This vision is summarised in St Bride's tagline under its logo: Creative, Progressive, Inclusive. In the seven years after the relaunch, the church gradually grew in activity and community engagement and now has a very supportive worshipping community. One of its enduring strengths, which the AI project clearly affirmed, was that St Bride's is a safe, sacred space for all.

St Bride's provides a home for a diverse range of community groups supporting people on the fringes of society, including those seeking refuge and asylum, and those living with mental distress, addiction and homelessness. Another element of the work is Open Table, a monthly

---

2 See a 2011 interview: https://www.theguardian.com/uk/the-northerner/2011/dec/08/liverpool-religion.

service for the Lesbian, Gay, Bisexual, Trans, Queer / Questioning, Intersex and Asexual (LGBTQIA+) community (see the Open Table story on page 78 for further information).

In 2014-15, as part of the church's celebration of seven years since its relaunch, the Rector invited Appreciating People to facilitate an AI process. Appreciating People (AP) helped the congregation to recognise its achievements and strengths, and co-create a shared vision for the next seven years. This invitation followed an effective AI project called *Count your Blessings* at St Michael's Church in the same deanery, six years earlier. The St Bride's project took place within the context of a Heritage Lottery Fund grant application to enable the building to be restored and made more accessible and flexible for community use.

The St Bride's community used Appreciative Inquiry (AI) to explore together as a church and wider community a vision for the next seven years, reviewing their existing 'Creative, Progressive, Inclusive' vision and to explore the future together.

Stage one: definition

This stage defined the project and its inquiry, identified hoped-for outcomes and project boundaries, and enabled key church and community participants to experience an AI process. It included:

- Initial meetings with the Rector considered the process and made initial plans including completing a successful funding proposal for the AI project.
- Two meetings with the Core Community (equivalent of a Parochial Church Council in the Church of England). The first meeting provided a practical AI experience, through a short workshop covering appreciative conversations, the use of visual minutes, and the possible project framework. The second meeting finalised the inquiry theme, the questions for the main appreciative conversation protocol, guidance on who should be interviewed, and the use of visual minuters to record events in a graphical way.
- Identifying with the Rector and Core Community (the internal project organisers) for the wider appreciative conversation process, with outline agreement to the questions and the people to be interviewed.
- The final step was to agree the timescale and Appreciating People's role in the project.

At the end of this process there was common agreement on an inquiry theme:
Creating Our Future Together: Reimagining St Bride's

Stage two: discovery

This stage had four elements:

1. Meetings with the AI project team to finalise the questions, manage the interview process and develop the interview support guidance and feedback arrangements.
2. A workshop after the Sunday morning service with the worshipping community, using three questions in paired conversations to enable people to experience an AI appreciative conversation.
3. A six-week process of appreciative conversations across the whole St Bride's community, and stakeholders, including the community groups which use the space, conducted by a number of interviewers supported by the AI project team. These were typically 45 minute interviews with up to eight questions allowing for a deeper response.
4. A report based on all the interview feedback, which would provide information for both stage four (see below) and for future investigation.

At the end of this process, 35+ people had taken part in the post worship conversation and 50+ had been involved in further appreciative conversations from across the worshipping community and groups who used the building. Significant information and knowledge gathered helped inform future needs and stages of the process.

People's honesty and openness provided a rich seam of thoughts and ideas. It proved to be a generative experience releasing energy and providing a positive framework for the next stage.

The themes which emerged at this stage were about St Bride's being a sanctuary where:

- informality encourages spiritual growth
- relationships and trust are central
- vulnerability is recognised, valued, and protected
- God's presence is experienced
- acceptance and welcome are key values

Stage three: discovery to dream

Appreciating People and the St Bride's AI project group co-designed an all day workshop for the St Bride's community using a combination of paired conversations and small group work which was visually minuted so that the community would have a permanent record of the process. The day revisited the themes from the stage three appreciative conversations, and included small group presentations of creative ideas for how St Bride's will operate in 2022 (seven years from the day of the workshop). Finally, the small groups began to identify future intentions. The community accepted that this element was a work in progress and would require further consideration at a later date.

> *Reflecting on the project outcomes at the end of the all-day workshop, it was noted that:*
>
> - *There was a sense of energy in the church and wider user groups;*
> - *High levels of engagement;*
> - *High levels of commitment from interviewers;*
> - *Useful information and in particular how St Bride's was important to individuals;*
> *Recognition of the positive journey St Bride's had been on in the last seven years in tune with its vision of creative/ progressive/ inclusive.*

Stage four: design and destiny interrupted

Basing the process on the 5D model, the project was about to enter the design stage. There was clear common ground across the worshipping community and user groups, and an identified need for further time for reflection to clarify the intentions and next steps. At this point, the St Bride's community expressed that the AI process:

- reconfirmed their creative, progressive and inclusive vision;
- had been valuable in supporting future plans;
- visual minutes provided both rich data and useful visual representation of the way forward.

After the September 2015 event, the St Bride's Core Community decided to review all the feedback from the complete AI process in four ways:

- **Discerning the future of the building:** A few days prior to the September 2015 event, the Core Community had become aware that a Heritage Lottery Fund grant they had been awarded was not going to be sufficient to undertake vital restoration and renovation of the church building. Although this serious situation was named during the process, the generative energy created in the meeting enabled the community to look beyond the issue and the building to the wider work and impact of St Bride's. In October 2015, the community held a 48-hour prayer vigil in which people were invited to reflect on three questions – not 'what shall we do with/without this building?' but:
  - What is God's work in this parish?
  - What ministries would support that work?
  - What resources would be required to support those ministries?

  After the prayer vigil, a community meeting reviewed feedback on these questions and made a majority decision to stay in the existing premises and find ways to raise the additional resources. Emerging from this event was the recognition that the AI process provided a generative effect and fostered resilience, providing clarity for the church and its future direction. The visual minutes and intentions created in the September 2015 event provided touchstones for the community as it made its decision, to ensure that what was decided was in keeping with those intentions, especially:

— What we do will be sustainable

— We will be a more open, beautiful and sacred space

— We will be an accessible, diverse community.

The building project group which emerged included members of the AI project team to ensure that the vision and intentions realised by the process are at the heart of new design proposals for the future of the building.

- **Practical tasks:** The Church Wardens reviewed all the appreciative conversations to identify practical tasks which could be prioritised in the short, medium and long term, or assessed as impractical due to availability of resources. These ranged from buying a new coffee machine (achievable in the short term) to constructing a labyrinth in the church grounds (potentially achievable in the long term depending on funding and work to regenerate the building).

- **Prophetic voice:** As Appreciating People facilitated the process, the community recognised that while there was a helpful process of drawing out common themes and values from the appreciative conversations there was also potential for what the Core Community called 'the prophetic voice'– a lone voice providing insight that others have missed – to be overlooked. In response the community set aside a small group to identify the prophetic voices.

Three members of the Core Community reviewed in depth all the significant information gathered between July and September 2015. They produced a report for the Core Community, and used quotes from the interviews to produce four poems which they presented at the church AGM in April 2016 and wove into the liturgy on the occasion of the anniversary of the start of the AI process in July 2016. By coincidence, this was the first Sunday after the departure of their Rector, and the beginning of the St Bride's community's reflection on its fears and hopes for the future as they discern who they will appoint to lead and build on the transformation they have shared since 2005.

The 'prophetic voice' group recognised that the AI appreciative conversations provided valuable insight into the ethos of the community that they wish to maintain and grow, and would inform the process of recruitment for a new Rector who could share and nurture this ethos.

Intentions and actions:

Two months on from the all day workshop in September 2016 during the morning service St Brides reflected on what had been achieved. Working in small groups they recorded some of their key thoughts and experiences.

The report below is to be adapted into a wall poster to remind the church community how far they have travelled.

"A safe sacred space for all"

> *"Appreciative Inquiry is a process for engaging people in building the kinds of organisations and a world they want to live in. Working from peoples' strengths and positive experiences, AI co-creates a future based on collaboration and open dialogue."*
>
> David Cooperrider, founder of Appreciative Inquiry

Introduction

During the Harvest Festival service, Tim at Appreciating People facilitated a conversation on the Appreciative Inquiry project and the journey from the September 2015 all church event. He reminded us of the context of what happened, and what Appreciative Inquiry is, based on David Cooperrider's quote. Using the metaphors below he helped people to consider the small and major things that have happened in these 12 months. He, also shared the story of Appreciative Inquiry and the Nepali village banks. How women in 1500 villages co-created the villages economic future and ran a small food bank to support village people.

Part one – context

Thoughts that were shared:

"Sharing the thoughts that it is 12 months from the September 2015 event and first stages of the Appreciative Inquiry project. Seeds were planted – ideas and shoots have emerged. People have continued to nurture and support the small growths. On occasions these plants have had to weather storms and cope with a changing environment. They still grow and flourish sometimes in the most surprising ways."

Part two – activity

In small groups people were asked to consider:

Considering the seeds planted and the shoots nurtured. What have we noticed that is different? What are the small steps we have and are taking? What has been our contribution no matter how small?

Part three – reflection

At the end of the group conversations people were asked to write down on Post-it notes some thoughts and phrases identifying the seeds and flourishing plants – the steps taken and noticing what is different.

Using flower shaped, leaf and butterfly Post-it notes, the comments were placed along the stems of a plant drawn on a flip chart, demonstrating large and small successes.

The information on the Post-it notes are provided verbatim and have not been prioritised.

- Pastoral care team- being there for one another
- The growth of open table x 4
- Soul friends' liturgy
- Make a joyful noise unto the Lord
- Just my beautiful 'selfs'
- FISH
- Sunday congregation more diverse
- BREWS
- A growing confidence... A deepening involvement
- Readings
- Book Group
- LGBT Christmas service
- Raising awareness of LGBTQIA issues
- Drawn heart shape
- Young people's soul group
- Diversity of ways for people to get involved in the community
- Give people a place to belong
- Food bank
- Soul friends
- The Growth of Soul friends groups
- The decision to stay in the building
- The WOW weekend away -----"WOW" (Parish weekend)

- Being available to people
- Growth of fair trade/ ethical products
- Open table
- Starting healing service
- Safe place
- Safe place to be
- Our community has grown with increased diversity
- Evolving inclusiveness
- Feeding back positive observations
- ART
- Prayer
- We're evolving all the time
- Deep listening
- St Bride's gift to the wider church though Appreciative Inquiry
- Format of the noticeboard has been improved
- Writing liturgies
- Deepening sense of belonging
- Improved use of space/ office/ fish/ tank/ storage
- Sense of belonging – tangible and intangible contributions
- Finding a voice... Greater awareness 'appreciation of our planet'
- Developing 'traidcraft' with others – new cupboard
- Finding a way to share what is important

❽ AI questions leading to effective actions and plans – What's your bag? Ideas from North Nibley chapel

This exercise needs pens, big sheets of paper, card, felt-tips, and a 'bag'....

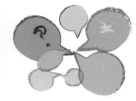

Suzanne Nockels from the Congregational Federation provides a practical example of how AI questions concentrated within the Discovery phase leads to effective actions and plans based on new insights into experience. People examined 'what works' and 'what we can do'.

The Congregational Church in North Nibley, Gloucester had closed, but a couple of people felt that it could be rejuvenated and re-opened. Lots of people within the Congregational Federation offered their support and expertise. The Area Worker, Rev Jill Stephen and the mission development officer had invested a great deal of time and things were moving.

I was invited to chair a one-off meeting about the future of the church. Up to that point villagers had plenty of ideas about what could happen in the building, but they hadn't really thought about what 'church' could look like or be. What is a church anyway? What are the core things in being a church? My brief was to begin a theological conversation. That was interesting given that the meeting was a mixture of past church members and interested villagers of all faiths and none.

We began with a large carpet bag. I drew out things that I carried everyday, including my car keys and a mobile phone and asked if anyone else had those things in their bag. I explained that, when my children were small, I carried some different items – like dummies – and I suspected that, as I grew older, I might carry other items. Church is like a bag... at different stages it might carry or contain different things but there might also be core things that it always possesses.

We then had paired conversations using the AI protocol style:

Q1   Tell me a story about a time when you've been aware of God/something bigger than yourself.

Q2   Where have you been aware of God/something bigger at work in North Nibley's story so far? It could be something big or small.

Q3   What do you hope <u>others</u> might discover from being part of North Nibley Church? What small thing might help with that?

Q4   What do <u>you</u> hope to discover from being part of North Nibley Church? What small thing might help with that?

Q5   What one thing could go into North Nibley's bag for the next stage of the journey? What does it symbolise?

This was followed by discussion in the whole group:
- How did you find the questions?
- What items do you think could go into the bag?
- What might a friend of North Nibley Congregational Church say is missing?
- How would you answer the question 'It would be great to learn more about...'

Two significant conversations happened in the course of the meeting. The first was a discussion about spirituality and prayer. The participants believed it was important and they wanted to get close to God, but were unsure how prayer worked or who could lead prayer.

They thought about what was simple and straightforward and how prayer could be woven into what they already planned to do. Rev Jill Stephen reported that, at their next planning meeting, someone spontaneously suggested they prayed about it.

Those gathered also spoke about the youth work that used to take place and how many young people had been positively influenced by it. One woman who was there because she was due to get married in the chapel, admitted to being a qualified youth worker and offered to help. Since that meeting, she has grown in other ways and is one of the central people in the church's development. Her offer at that time gave people hope.

North Nibley Chapel is currently a vibrant community hub offering Messy Church and other forms of worship.

⑨ Methodist Summer School chaplaincy and vocation

Matthew Reed and Lynne Norman from the Methodist Church offer an example that demonstrates the weaving of AI tools into a wider programme and how the process can support reflective and spiritual practices.

Delivering a summer school at Cliff College on the subject of chaplaincy and vocation, Matthew Reed and Lynne Norman, two members of Methodist Church staff, used Appreciative Inquiry as part of the programme. They found a SOAR™ exercise particularly effective during a session exploring individual calling.

They started by explaining that – unlike other areas of the course – the session would feature very little in the way of 'from-the-front' teaching. They believed it was important to allow time for participants to reflect on learning so far (at the end of the second day of a five-day week), as well as giving them space to really listen to God and to their own inner voice. The students were encouraged to approach this session in an attitude of prayer.

After explaining the principles behind a SOAR™ exercise and a reading from Luke 10: 1–11 (Jesus sends out the seventy-two), the students were given a specially adapted SOAR™ worksheet and allowed 20 minutes to complete it in quiet contemplation. Questions on the SOAR™ included reflections on the Bible reading, such as, 'Where are the places that "Christ himself might intend to go?"' and 'What might sharing peace mean?' Another question, under the 'strengths' heading and reflecting on earlier teaching, was 'Considering the story of Martin of Tours, the first chaplain, who tore his cloak in half to share with a man in need, what is your cloak? What do you offer?'

After 20 minutes, the group was led into a time focusing on the Methodist Covenant Prayer. Participants were encouraged to 'settle into' the prayer as it was read through, becoming aware of the presence of God and then remaining in an attitude of quiet contemplation as questions for reflection and prompts for private prayer were slowly read aloud. Following this, and in recognition of the fact that the extroverts in the room may have reached their capacity for silent thinking, the group was offered a number of options for the remainder of the session. Participants could continue work on their SOAR™; approach one of the tutors for one-on-one conversation and prayer; approach a fellow student and work in pairs to go through an appreciative conversation worksheet; or could simply work through the appreciative questions on their own. Some people took the opportunity to escape the room – to either have the conversation or find space for personal reflection – but many stayed in the room and the atmosphere was one of deep prayer and meditation.

At the end of the session, several students approached Matthew, Lynne and the other course tutor and most had been positively affected by the experience. One student said that he had tried vocational exercises before, including a SOAR™, but had never found them useful until now. He felt the fact the activity had been framed in prayer and in the Bible, had really helped him. Others simply expressed an appreciation of the fact they had been given time to think and reflect in a very busy week. One or two were very keen to book time with the course tutors to discuss what they had discovered about themselves during the session.

This is an alternative to a SWOT analysis (strengths, weaknesses, opportunities, threats). While a SWOT is great for practical tasks (like building a house), the threats and weaknesses tend to dominate.

A SOAR™ exercise is visionary and also helps to identify measures of success.

After reading the Bible passage below, use the questions in the table as a guide to complete the exercise. You can draw images or write bullet points – it's up to you. Sometimes it helps to complete the aspirations before the opportunities. Review your SOAR™ regularly.

Luke 10: 1 – 11 (New International Version)

Jesus sends out the seventy-two

After this the Lord appointed 72 others and sent them two by two ahead of him to every town and place where he was about to go. [2] He told them, 'The harvest is plentiful, but the workers are few. Ask the Lord of the harvest, therefore, to send out workers into his harvest field. [3] Go! I am sending you out like lambs among wolves. [4] Do not take a purse or bag or sandals; and do not greet anyone on the road.

[5] 'When you enter a house, first say, "Peace to this house." [6] If someone who promotes peace is there, your peace will rest on them; if not, it will return to you. [7] Stay there, eating and drinking whatever they give you, for the worker deserves his wages. Do not move around from house to house.

[8] 'When you enter a town and are welcomed, eat what is offered to you. [9] Heal the sick who are there and tell them, "The kingdom of God has come near to you." [10] But when you enter a town and are not welcomed, go into its streets and say, [11] "Even the dust of your town we wipe from our feet as a warning to you. Yet be sure of this: The kingdom of God has come near."'

SOAR™ exercise handout personal SOAR™ (strengths, opportunities, aspirations, results/ resources).

Strengths	Opportunities
Considering the story of Martin of Tours, the first chaplain, who tore his cloak in half to share with a man in need, what is your cloak? What do you offer? What are you good at? What skills and special knowledge do you have? What do other people appreciate about you? What are the strengths in your day to day spiritual journey? What do you value most in your spiritual life?	What opportunities can help build your skills and strengths? How can you utilise the skills and strengths you have? What do you feel it is that you HAVE to do? Who can help you on your journey? How does/can your faith and spiritual practice support you in your daily life? How can you utilise them more effectively? How can you build on your existing spiritual practice? Who can help you in your spiritual/vocational journey?
Aspirations	**Resources/Results (can use either)**
What's your passion? What hopes do you have for your future spiritual journey? What do you want to achieve? What would it look like if you achieved it? What would a vocational expression of your spiritual life look like? What 'itch' do you need to scratch? Considering Luke 10: 1 – 11, where are the places that Christ himself might intend to go? What might sharing peace mean? What might it mean to heal the sick?	What resources do you need to meet your aspirations and maximise your opportunities? What are the first 2 things you need to do? How would you measure success and celebrate your achievements? What resources do you need to help you in your spiritual journey and to further explore your calling? How will you know that your spiritual life has grown and deepened? Considering Luke 10: 1 – 11, what would 'travelling light' mean?

Appreciative interview – thinking differently

Working either in pairs, or on your own if you prefer, take it in turns to ask the following questions. Be aware of listening carefully to each other, and not adding in your own story.

1. Share something that you have really enjoyed in your working life (could be a volunteer or learning experience) – something that stood out for you. Tell it as a story...
2. What is the one thing you do that you really enjoy doing?
3. What one thing do you do that others seem to really appreciate? What do other people tell you that you should be doing?
4. Is there something that you keep coming back to in your working life (perhaps even when you've tried to ignore or dismiss it)?
5. Have you ever turned down an opportunity and then regretted it or felt an uneasy feeling that you should have taken it up?

Reflecting on the Covenant Prayer (see below), you could also explore the following questions:

1. What jumps out at you?
2. What would you find easy to say?
3. What would you find difficult to say?
4. What things might God be asking you to stop?
5. What might God be asking you to continue?
6. And what new things may God place in your life?

Methodist Covenant prayer, adapted by John Wesley

I am no longer my own but yours.
Put me to what you will, rank me with whom you will;
put me to doing, put me to suffering;
let me be employed for you, or laid aside for you,
exalted for you, or brought low for you;
let me be full, let me be empty,
let me have all things, let me have nothing:
I freely and wholeheartedly yield all things to your pleasure and disposal.
And now, glorious and blessèd God, Father, Son and Holy Spirit,
you are mine and I am yours. So be it.
And the covenant now made on earth, let it be ratified in heaven

⑩ Appreciating Open Table: creating an inclusive, safe, sacred space to 'come as you are'

This is an example of using elements of the AI 5D process such as discovery, dream, design to help plan the way forward for a group. Warren Hartley and Kieran Bohan describe how the event concentrated on identifying core principles for the group through collaboration from all the participants. It is an example of co-designing and co-creating.

Context: St Bride's Liverpool relaunched in November 2007, with a vision for a 'creative, progressive, inclusive' church (see page 68). Open Table (OT) began in July 2008 as a manifestation of this vision. OT aims to create a safe, sacred space for Lesbian, Gay, Bisexual, Trans, Queer/Questioning, Intersex and Asexual (LGBTQIA+) people, who often feel unwelcome in mainstream churches.[3]

At an early meeting, a member asked: 'Will it be "open table", welcoming everyone to share the Eucharist?' We felt this was at the heart of why this community was needed, as LGBTQIA+ Christians have often felt excluded or been intentionally excluded from the Eucharist. So the OT ecumenical worshipping community began as a monthly Eucharist, with a mix of Anglicans, Roman Catholics, United Reformed Church and Methodist folk.

Our goal is to explore faith amongst LGBTQIA+ Christians, and assist them in integrating their spiritual, sexual or gender identities. For some these identities have been in direct conflict with one another. We also welcome family members, friends and all who believe in an inclusive church.

To create this sacred space where all can 'come as you are', we carefully choose liturgical resources that affirm our identity as children of God. Participation in the monthly Eucharist has grown from six in 2008 up to 40 in 2016. We also gather for sharing circles, house groups and retreats, and now meet on another Sunday in the month for a bring and share agape meal.

In 2015, other OT gatherings emerged, and as we write, there are also OT communities in Warrington, Manchester and north Wales, with enquiries from other communities nationally. Each is independent, whilst we offer support and encouragement from our experience.

In March 2016, the Archdeacon of Liverpool commissioned us both as Local Missional Leaders for three years to develop this ministry. We needed to make a plan for developing OT in Liverpool, and to ensure that emerging OT communities are safe, sustainable, and share this vision. We approached Appreciating People to co-facilitate an 'Appreciating OT day' to enable this community development.

We agreed the desired outcomes of the day were to identify:
* What OT does well;
* How OT contributes to people's spiritual life;
* The core values of OT;
* What OT needs to do differently;
* Practical guidelines for developing OT, especially in new communities.

We briefed each OT community's leadership to identify people who wanted to take part, and tried out questions that became part of the final protocol:

Appreciative questions

Q1   Think of a time or experience when your involvement with Open Table has made a difference to you. Please share it as a story.

Q2   How does the Open Table community support and feed your spiritual life? It can be the smallest thing.

Q3   What do you think the core values of Open Table are/ should be?

Q4   In your experience what does the Open Table community do really well?

Q5   What do you think needs to be done differently to make the Open Table community even better?

Q6   What simple step or action could Open Table do to help you?

Q7   How could you help Open Table? It can be the smallest thing.

---

3   For more about Open Table, visit opentable.lgbt and for a short history of it see Journeys In Grace & Truth ed. Jayne Ozanne (Via Media, 2016).

24 members of OT communities in Liverpool, Manchester, Warrington and North Wales came together on the day. We interviewed six people beforehand who could not attend, and shared quotes from their conversations:

- 'The level of genuine excitement to see me was breath-taking';
- 'People can come with no fear and be completely themselves, to worship God with like-minded people. You can be closer to God when others accept you';
- 'I've felt comfortable inviting friends and family to join us at OT no matter what their beliefs, sexuality, gender or background'.

As OT is a dispersed community, some had not met before. We invited people to pair with someone they would like to know better. Here is a sample of answers to two 'firestarter' questions:

Why is OT important to you?

Comment	Theme this suggests
A really intentional and successfully welcoming community, warm and friendly	Welcome and hospitality
Safe place to be honest: to myself, my community, God	Safety
Supportive. Accepted me. Let me know it's fine to be a gay Christian	Acceptance and inclusion
Finally able to attend church and not have to lie!	Honesty and integrity
Made friends, broadened my spiritual life. 'OT has been my family, helped me come out, and meet diverse people.'	Friendship and family
Fresh and just view, opportunity for the church	Spirituality and opportunity

What do you hope we will achieve today?

Comment	Theme this suggests
I hope to set up my own OT: to be able to present a set of values and ideas for an OT structure to the church will be great!	Growth and potential
Clear OT values and vision for the future	Clarity
To discern God's will for OT and ensure voices are heard in a safe and affirming way	Spiritual discernment
Working out core values and how they can be spread	Common ground / shared learning

Participants completed the seven questions above in paired conversations, then formed groups of six to identify common themes about how OT makes a difference to them, supports their spiritual life, and is underpinned by core values.

How OT makes a difference:

Comment	Theme this suggests
Good to feel accepted, respected, welcome as I am	Welcome and hospitality
Gives a safe space so we are able to grow	Safety
Affirming, valued, accepted	Acceptance and inclusion
Don't have to hide yourself	Honesty and integrity
Being asked to do tasks helps me feel valued	Empowerment
Helped me bring others back to faith	Spirituality and opportunity

How OT supports your spiritual life:

Comment	Theme this suggests
Stays there for us	Safety and sustainability
Really improved my prayer life – getting used to open prayer	Openness
Giving & receiving love – all descending from God	Loving and engaging
Opening up scripture – looking at wider picture	Scripture
Helps me understand we are all created in God's image, regardless of sexuality or gender	Inclusivity and integration
Crucial that we are able to be truthful about ourselves	Honesty and integrity

OT core values:

- Safe sacred space;
- Spiritual, God-centred;
- Open, accessible;
- Accepting and inclusive;
- Welcoming and inviting;
- Sincere, respectful, non-judgmental;
- Eucharistic and ecumenical;
- Empowering;
- Care for all ages;
- Integrating the whole person – body/ mind/ spirit;
- Empathy and solidarity;
- Celebrate and value diversity.

We led a guided meditation where we asked participants to imagine that it is summer 2019 and we have gathered to celebrate the OT community. Then each group were asked to discuss and share their vision of:

- What is different?
- What were the challenges?
- What have we achieved?
- How have we helped people?

One group presented through drama how OT helps people by being holistic – bringing body, mind and spirit together to celebrate our lives as beloved children of God.

A second group portrayed people from diverse OT communities gathered under one large rainbow umbrella, with the slogan, 'All different, all together'.

A third group showed a row of people connected together like pylons, linked with 'power lines' of shared values. They predicted that in 2019:

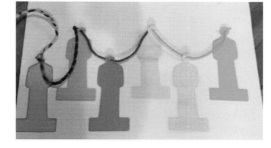

- Both CofE and URC support same-sex marriage;
- Larger number of OT groups with regional committees;
- Movement towards integration with mainstream church;
- Informing training on gender and sexuality in ministerial formation.

The last group portrayed an OT LGBTQIA+ Christian community festival, with a storm cloud for challenges faced, and a rainbow for our diversity and achievements.

Finally we asked for guidelines that the participants would suggest to OT groups, especially those newly emerging. They suggested:

- An affirming host community;
- Safe space;
- Accessible e.g. transport;
- Continuity of time and place;
- Host church stays true to itself and wider OT values
- Take advantage of OT network support, guidance and accountability;
- Listen and be open minded;
- Use inclusive language in liturgy and in speaking with people;
- Make sure all are fed;
- Respond to local needs and abilities;
- Think globally, act locally;
- Be clear about use of money – avoid financial pressure to contribute

Next steps: The next month, our Eucharist liturgy included quotes from the paired appreciative conversations, which we shared with other OT facilitators for use in worship.

⑪ Shaping the Vestry Prayer

AI can influence all areas of church life, including prayer. An example is this set of prompts for the vestry prayer, said with and for the preacher by one of the elders before the Sunday morning service in many churches. This guideline, offered by Matthew Reed, emerged from the Methodist Church Discipleship, Ministries and Learning Network.

In an early pilot of a training scheme for lay church officers, a colleague identified the Vestry Prayer as a pinch-point for lay people understanding the spiritual implications and obligations of supporting worship. From that starting point we developed an AI based prayer writing exercise to fulfil this learning objective.

In the Methodist tradition (and many others) the duty steward leads the preacher in a personal prayer before they go in to lead worship. For many stewards, this is the first time they are called on to lead prayer in any way that involves them consciously contributing to the spiritual life of the Church and, in turn, highlights a spiritual responsibility to the whole worshipping community.

This short activity was designed to help stewards to craft the vestry prayer. It involves an AI protocol of four questions, each of three parts, which leads to a simple four-line prayer.

The outcome for the stewards undertaking the training was to engage in deep thinking and personal prayer, leading to a highly personal prayer of their own creation. The realisation that they could do this was hugely significant, while for some it was important to understand that they were *allowed* to do it was shock. In the training session we found that some actually wrote a prayer, while others talked about their experience of what has happened in the past – either outcome was beneficial.

For us as leaders of the course (and preparing the AI protocol) it was deeply rewarding to see how people who tended to see worship as something they received, turned into something that they expected to contribute to creatively: people who expected to be organising, or following a checklist of duties, were now able to see their role as directly connected to serving God.

Perhaps more significantly, some of those who participated have gone on to use this approach in writing a new prayer for each occasion they are on duty, and preachers have noted how important it is for them to have more personal, pertinent and distinctive prayer as this critical moment in worship preparation.

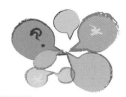

Protocol for an individual appreciative conversation about worship

The act of worship

- What is this act of worship for?
- What is the best thing you want from this act of worship personally?
- What can you ask God to do?

The preacher

- What might the preacher be feeling at this point?
- What is the best thing that they could feel?
- What can you ask God to do?

The congregation

- What does the congregation need and want?
- What is the best that could happen to them in the service?
- What can you ask God to do?

God

- What might God want from this act of worship?
- What is the best we can offer?
- What can you ask God to do?

3

AI resources, guidance and tasks

PART THREE
AI resources, guidance and tasks

In parts two and three, you will have noticed guidance on using the AI approach as well as examples of AI protocols, exercises and helpful hints.

Here are more materials and activities to provide ideas for your AI practice. Some are drawn from the AI in Action examples in Part two and others from Appreciating People's experience:

a.   Appreciative conversation protocols and guidance to interviewers;

b.   The importance of reframing;

c.   Additional guidance on the 5D framework, the AI summit and ARE IN;

d.   SOAR™ examples and further guidance;

e.   Advice and activities for introducing AI into meetings;

f.   Importance of appreciative journaling to your AI practice;

g.   Appreciative feedback and simple evaluation activities.

❶ Appreciative conversation protocols and guidance to interviewers

> These three examples of appreciative conversation protocols, have been developed for use in church and community settings.

Appreciative conversations: a long protocol version

The format below is a standard protocol which can be used for paired conversations as part of a church development plan. When used in AI training, these protocols are also often given as a handout with space included to make legible notes where the paired conversation is peer-to-peer, in which case the listener's notes are given to the speaker at the end of the conversation. Such formatting has been shown for the first example. When you draft a protocol, leave a few spaces between the questions, especially if you are not using a feedback sheet.

Guidance for appreciative conversations/interviews

Appreciative conversations are different from traditional interviews in that the questions concentrate on, 'what works'. They look at problems and issues from a different perspective by focusing on the generative and creative. Just record the key themes, story elements and quotes in the space provided.

Helpful hints

To help support the conversation, learn more about each other and go deeper into responses, it is helpful to ask supplementary questions such as:

Q. Tell me more?

Q. Who else was involved?

Q. What were you thinking?

Q. How did it feel?

Appreciative questions

Q1 Think of a time or experience when your involvement and engagement with this church has made a difference to you. Share it as a story.

Q2 How would you describe your involvement with this church and community?

Q3 How does this church community support and feed your spiritual life. It can be the smallest thing. (Only use this if appropriate).

Q4 What is special about this place and the people involved?

Q5 In your experience, what does this church and its community do really well?

Q6 What do you think needs to be done differently to make this church community even better?

Q7 It is spring 2022 and we are meeting to celebrate our journey together.

- What is different?
- What has been achieved?
- What are the challenges that have been overcome?
- Describe it as if it has happened and explain it in as much detail as you can.

Q8 What could help move the work forward?

- Describe one small step; describe one challenging or radical action

Feedback form

A standard feedback form for AI conversations, normally when appreciative conversations are held prior to a large group event. It is a generic one based on the St Bride's experience. The form draws on questions from the first example protocol...

Appreciative conversation feedback sheet

Name of interviewee (optional): _____

Date: _____

Group or Interviewer: _____

Guidance

Please record stories, any emerging themes and great quotes (please obtain agreement to share quotes and stories.) Recording comments as bullet points can be helpful...

Stories/quotes about what has made a difference (question 1)

Involvement in the church and community (question 2)

Supporting your spiritual life and special place/ people (questions 3 and 4)

What does this church and community do well? (question 5)

What needs to be done differently? (question 6)

What is different about this place in 2022? (question 7)
Any comments:

Guidance to interviewers for a church and/ or wider community engagement process, used to support the conversations across the church community and people/ groups who use the meeting spaces. Based on the St Bride's project.

Example two

This example is drawn from the St Bride's project and is the protocol used after morning worship in the Discovery stage of the process (see page 69).

The protocol's purpose is to find out why the church is important to the participant, what it does well and to suggest possible further simple actions.

1. Share a story or experience about a time when being part of this church has been important and made a difference in your life (it can be something small).
2. What is special about this place and its people?
3. What does this church do really well?
4. What would make this church a even better place and community? Think of a small step...

At the end of the conversation, participants were asked to record any key points on Post-it notes and then these were shared on a large noticeboard. Displaying them and reading some of them out loud was found to be a powerful and energising experience for the people present.

Example three

Appreciative conversation – an example of a protocol for the URC Church Life Review project

This protocol is part of the emerging Church Life Review prototype being co-created with a number of URC congregations in the Yorkshire Synod. It is at a draft stage and is going through further testing.

Questions

1. Tell us about a time or experience when being part of this church community has made a difference to you in both your personal and spiritual life (describe it as a story; who was involved, what happened and how did make a difference?)

2. Could you tell us what is special about this church community for you and what does it do well?

3. In what ways does the life and work of this church help you on your spiritual journey?

4. What things do you think we should talk about to help our church move forward?

5. What are the ways your church helps you see God's work in every day life?

6. What are the ways this church helps others and the wider community see God's work in every day life?

7. How can this Church Life Review help you and your church?

8. It is 18 months after the Church Life Review was completed and the church is meeting to reflect on what is different and how have the challenges identified and actions required been met. Celebrating the achievements. Describe it as if it has happened.

9. What for you would be the smallest actions that could be taken to support this church's next steps?

Thanks for taking part and contributing to this project.

Guidance to interviewers for a church and/ or wider community engagement process, used to support the conversations across the church community and people/ groups who use the meeting spaces.

Dear ...

This church is reviewing its future and would like you to be part of it.

Would you be willing to be an interviewer / interviewed* as part of this process over the next month?

Delete as appropriate.

To help us achieve this, we are looking for volunteers to interview people / be interviewed* about their experience of being part of this church community, using an 'appreciative conversation framework'. An appreciative conversation framework is a set of structured questions to help us inquire more deeply into the life of this church community in all its forms. These structured conversations will help us to discover the strengths of the people and groups that are part of this church and 'what works', so that together we can develop them for everyone's benefit.

Becoming an interviewer
Being an interviewer involves arranging a one-to-one meeting with a member of one or more of the groups that meet at this church for around 30 minutes, asking them a series of short questions about their experience of us, recording brief notes and observations on the interview and feeding it back.

A useful definition:

'AI is a process for engaging people in building the kinds of organisations and a world they want to live in. Working from people's strengths and positive experiences, AI co-creates a future based on collaboration and dialogue'

David Cooperrider, creator of AI.

It's important to remember that AI is about how we both individually and collectively create change; it's about taking problems seriously by looking at them differently.

❷ The importance of reframing

Reframing is an important process in both designing and delivering appreciative conversations. The guidance given here is drawn from two sources: *How to be More Awesome* and development of an exercise during *Appreciating Church* training courses. Responses are always very different when using this exercise, and sharing ideas is a major part of the learning.

Positive psychology studies of the brain show that focusing on problems triggers our brain's fear responses, lowering our ability to find solutions. Positive emotions, such as joy and contentment, broaden thought–action repertoire, expanding the range of behaviours – these broadened mindsets build an individual's resources. So it pays to observe unhelpful, limiting thoughts and replace them with more positive thoughts and perspectives.

A picture can look very different according to the frame it is put in. Reframing allows us to take any situation or experience and view it through a different lens – or place it in an alternative 'frame'. Deliberate and conscious positive reframing draws on the AI principles and allows us to view our experience in a new light. It is a powerful way to transform our thinking and supports resilience and creativity. Are you 'broadening and building' or 'narrowing' your response options?

An easy way to practice reframing is by noticing the language that we use, and to soften it, for instance – *'I don't have enough qualifications'* can be reframed into *'how can I improve my learning and qualifications?'*

Ask about the underlying enthusiasm or wish and explore what might be unexpressed. For example, consider, *'what might we want more of?'* or *'how might we have succeeded in the past?'* If someone says *'worship services are boring'* then reframe by asking: *'what would make services interesting?'*

Reframing in practice

This exercise was developed as part of the *Appreciating Church* Taste of AI programme and available to download from: www.appreciating.church.

Group reframing exercise for congregation/ Quaker meeting/ church body

Reframing involves noticing how we see something and choosing to see it differently; just as a picture can be transformed by changing the frame that it's in. It plays a key role in appreciative conversations and elsewhere in Appreciative Inquiry methods.

Task: In small groups, consider the issues and matters in the left hand column; then reframe and compose possible options in the right hand column. There might be a number of options. The first one has begun to be addressed as a prompt. Choose the issues which are most relevant to your situation at the present time.

At the end of the exercise, reflect on the experience of reframing each issue – possible answers can be shared in the large group. Remember that there are multiple ways of reframing and each suggestion can provide a useful basis for creative discussion.

Issues and/ or concerns	Reframe (there could be a number of alternatives)
The church building is too big for the congregation	A building that meets our needs What kind of space would work well for us?
Our youth group always makes a mess of the church hall	
We haven't got enough ministry to go round	
Why won't anyone offer to be an elder/ deacon/ lay leader etc?	
Where are the young families?	
Our worshipping community is getting smaller	
The minister and the congregation are out of step with one another	
The people who take an active part in the life of the church/ congregation/ meeting are ageing	
I don't feel welcome here	
People keep stopping us from trying new things	
We tried that once and it didn't work	

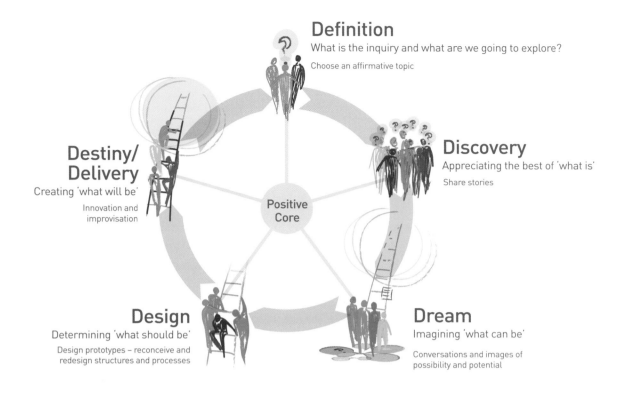

Definition
What is the inquiry and what are we going to explore?
Choose an affirmative topic

Discovery
Appreciating the best of 'what is'
Share stories

Destiny/ Delivery
Creating 'what will be'
Innovation and improvisation

Positive Core

Design
Determining 'what should be'
Design prototypes – reconceive and redesign structures and processes

Dream
Imagining 'what can be'
Conversations and images of possibility and potential

❸ Guidance on the 5D framework, the AI summit and additional tools

Included here are a short description of the AI summit process, explanation of the ARE IN tool and its role in the definition phase; useful tools for design and destiny including prototyping, and further explanation of 'intentions'.

AI summit

The AI summit is a large group method for accelerating positive change in organisations and communities, through involving a broad range of internal and external stakeholders. It is typically a single event or series of events (usually three to five days in length), that brings people together to:

1. Discover the organisation or community's core competencies and strengths;

2. Envision opportunities for positive change;

3. Design the desired changes into the organisation or communities' systems, structures, strategies and cultures;

4. Implement, and sustain the changes and make them work.

AI summits range from 30 to 3,000 people and can include more by using online technology. A summit uses the 5D framework as a model, drawing on support and planning groups in many situations to bring the whole system together. If it is not possible to hold the summit as a single event, there are other ways of undertaking the approach. Examples include using one day for discovery and dream and establishing task and finish groups for design and destiny, or undertaking discovery prior to an event and using a day event to complete dream,design and destiny. The summit process has been used widely in the corporate sector.

For further information summits go to the internet and look for examples. *The Appreciative Inquiry Summit – a practitioner's guide for leading large group change* is a useful book.

(James D. Ludema, Diana Whitney, Bernard J. Mohr and Thomas J. Griffin; Berrett-Koehler, 2003)

ARE IN

One of the challenges in bringing the whole system together to explore an organisation's development plans is to ensure you have got the 'right' people there. A useful tool for this is the ARE IN tool, created by Marvin Weisbord and Sandra Janoff, as part of the 'Futuresearch' model[1]. They recommend that a whole system event or process being developed within an organisation or community should include participants who 'ARE IN', i.e. those with:

A uthority to act (e.g. decision making responsibility in an organisation or community);

R esources such as contacts, time or, money;

E xpertise in the issues to be considered;

I nformation about the topic that no others have;

N eed to be involved because they will be affected by the outcome and can speak to the consequences;

'ARE IN' could be a useful mechanism to ensure buy-in and ownership when planning a large scale AI intervention.

Instead of formal delivery plans, try using intentions with simple action plans with an annual review cycle based on a short appreciative conversation.

❹ SOAR ™ – examples and further guidance

Further to the SOAR™ information on page 45, and the spiritual SOAR™ model on page 46, here are some examples of SOAR™ approaches. Traditionally, SOAR™ has taken place in the design phase. More recently, it is being used as a standalone tool. We've included examples for teams, an AI practitioner and a church development plan.

SOAR™ exercises can be undertaken in a variety of ways:

- Individually and then shared and fine tuned in pairs: peer-to-peer coaching;
- In a small group, using the questions to guide the conversation – a kind of protocol;
- In a small group, where one person completes the task and other group members act as advisers – the consultant approach.

Helpful hints

When completing a SOAR™ exercise, take either A4 or A3 paper, mark it into quadrants, with S, O, A and R heading each one respectively. R denotes either resources and/or results, depending on the context you're using it in. Going through each stage logically is not required as sometimes it is helpful, for example, to go to aspirations before opportunities – this can help identify more opportunities later. The questions provided are just for guidance – feel free to add or delete where necessary. Add SOAR™ examples to your church plans and funding applications.

1 'Don't Just Do Something stand there! 10 principles for leading meetings that Matter': Marvin Weisbord and Sandra Janoff, Berret Koehler 2007

Example one: TEAM SOAR™

A SOAR™ tool for small teams wishing to explore and co-create their future.

Strengths	Opportunities
What does the team do well? What are its successes when it is working at its best? What are the top five strengths in the team? What are the skills, knowledge and expertise team members could contribute more of? What have been the major achievements?	What are the existing opportunities for this team to flourish? What are the opportunities internally that can be utilised more? Who can help you? In what ways can other people/ colleagues support you? What are the innovative opportunities this team could work on?
Aspirations	**Resources/Results**
What is the passion and motivation of this team? What does this team aspire to do more of? What successes/ changes might you in see the team in 12 months' time? What new ways of working/ providing services might you see in the organisation over the next 18 months?	What are the resources needed to move forward? What are the first steps and smallest actions you can take? What would be the most innovative? How will you know you've got there? What will it look like?

Example two – a church/ meeting development plan SOAR™

Here is SOAR™ employed as a tool for co-designing a church plan. It could be used either as part of a church meeting, or with individuals.

Strengths	Opportunities
What are the existing strengths of this church and its people? What skills, knowledge and experience do we bring to this church and its people? Why is this church important to people? What does the congregation/ meeting do well? What have we done well and made a difference? How do we support people in their spiritual life?	What are the opportunities for this church to flourish? What are the opportunities internally that could be used more effectively? What are the opportunities for our spiritual life to grow? What can we learn from other churches?
Aspirations	**Resources/Results**
What new ways of working do we need to create to fulfil God's purpose? In what ways do we want this church/ meeting to develop and achieve?	What are the resources needed to help us move forward? Who can we call on for help and support? What are the first steps and smallest actions? How will we know we have got there? What will it look like? How will the church identify and recognise the results?

Example three – A SOAR™ for the AI practitioner journey

This uses SOAR™ as a reflective and learning tool, designed to support your AI journey.
We suggest it's done twice a year. This is an exercise undertaken during the *Appreciating Church*
Advanced AI programme: *Developing Your AI Practice.*

Strengths	Opportunities
What are the best parts of your current AI activities? When do you know you have been effective? What are the skills and strengths you bring to your AI journey? What do you value about your AI work? What are other experiences and skills you blend into your AI practice?	What are the opportunities out there for your AI to flourish? Which of your AI strengths and skills could you develop? How can you maximise and utilise the opportunities out there? What AI experiences do you wish to explore and learn more about?
Aspirations	Resources/Results
Why are you passionate about AI? What more do you want to do with your AI work? It's two years' time and you are reflecting on your AI journey to this point. What is different and what have you achieved? What do you need to do differently with your AI practice?	How will you know your AI experience and knowledge is increasing? What is the smallest action you need to do? What is the most innovative step? How will you recognise your AI skills and experience has increased? How will you know that your AI experience and knowledge is making a difference?

❺ Advice and activities for introducing AI into meetings

In the AI journey, it's important to realise that AI is not just a set of management tools, although they are useful and appropriate on many occasions. It can be transformational to blend AI-type questions and conversations into a range of existing organisational practices. Adding a paired conversation during a meeting and including generative questions can encourage positivity and co-creation. Below are examples you can use in various situations. Try them, observe and then reflect what happens.

- When this organisation was working really well what were we doing?
- When we had a problem and successfully resolved it what did we do?
- When we are successful what does it look like and how do we celebrate it?
- What existing strengths and skills could we use more effectively to support this organisation/ group/ team/ church?
- What do we need to do differently?
- How can we involve everybody?
- What are we learning from what is not working?

Running meetings with a difference

These suggestions are based on practical experience.

Consider changing the agenda so that minutes and matters arising are placed in the middle or at the end of the meeting. Discuss and agree the most important items and do them first. This will always give more time to the essential business and can help animate participants.

Start your meetings with simple exercises such as:

- Asking each participant to answer: *'what would be the best thing to come out of this meeting?' 'What, for you, would make this meeting a success?' 'Since our last meeting what have we achieved? It can be a small thing...' 'What is the most important thing we need to address?'*

End the meeting with simple exercises, such as:

- Ask each participant to write down on a Post-it note the one action they will do to help deliver the agreed actions. Ask questions like: *'what has been the most important thing we have achieved to today?' 'Have we met your meeting intentions you raised at the beginning?' 'What have we enjoyed and found valuable?'*

During the meeting, suggest exploring agenda items by breaking into pairs with a question on one of the topics, and then feeding back. If the group is large, move the pairs into sixes after the paired conversation and then do group feedback.

Impact

These ideas foster better engagement, wider conversations, support creativity and make meetings more enjoyable.

❻ The importance of journaling to your Appreciative Inquiry practice

Appreciative journaling is an excellent way to embed the philosophy of AI, and keeping an appreciative journal is a key practical element in *Appreciating Church* and training programmes. It's invaluable in developing your appreciative muscle, practising your appreciative skills, and supporting wellbeing, flourishing and resilience. All participants on the *Appreciating Church* training receive an appreciative journal and are encouraged to use it as part of their post course support and work programme. It is a requirement for people working towards accreditation as an *Appreciating Church* trainer, facilitator or coach.

- Creating and using a journal contributes to your wellbeing, by making you more appreciative of yourself, others, and the world around you.
- It has been shown that optimistic thinking increases a variety of physical attributes including life expectancy[2]. Journaling about one positive experience from the previous 24 hours allows your brain to relive it and you to receive the benefits [3].

Journal exercise

A simple way to start journaling is to use a note book and undertake the following exercise

(You may prefer to take photographs, draw pictures, or make a voice recording. The point is to keep a record in the form that works for you of your observations over 28 days.)

For 28 days, write down three good things that happened to you on each day. They can be small – like a cup of coffee or a conversation. Then consider:

- Why did this good thing happen?
- What does it mean to me?
- How can I have more of it?

At the end of the 28 days, read through what you have recorded and answer these questions, adding them to your note book:

Q: What have you enjoyed about the process and how has it helped you?

Q: What have you learned about yourself?

Q: What are the changes you have noticed?

Examen – The spiritual tradition of journaling

The spiritual tradition of journaling is exemplified by the Examen spiritual exercises developed by the Jesuit founder Ignatius of Loyola (1491-1556).

Kieran Bohan, Mission Enabler at St Bride's in Liverpool discusses the use of this below:

The Examen is designed to be practiced daily. Ignatius of Loyola wrote The Spiritual Exercises[4], which have been a guide for people making spiritual retreats since the 16th century. The exercises begin by recommending that everyone be taught the Examen. Ignatius saw the Examen as the cornerstone of the spiritual life to the extent that when the Jesuits at the Council of Trent asked if they could skip their prayer exercises because they had no time, Ignatius told them to skip anything but the Examen.

Regular practice of the Examen can reveal a direction for our life – the Examen is what changed Ignatius from a wild soldier to a pilgrim walking barefoot to Jerusalem. He believed that, as we are made in God's image and likeness (Genesis 1:27), by reflecting regularly on our desires, the Examen can help to put us in touch with the voice of God that is within each one of us.

He taught that God speaks through our deepest feelings and yearnings, what he called 'consolation' and 'desolation.' Consolation is whatever helps us connect with ourselves, others, God and the universe. Desolation is whatever disconnects us. Ignatius recommended returning to

---

2 (Jackie Kelm, *Appreciative Living*)
3 Shawn Achor, *The happy secret to better work* www.ted.com/talks/lang/en/shawn_achor_the_happy_secret_to_better_work.html
4 The *Spiritual Exercises* of Ignatius of Loyola, 1650

our deepest moments of consolation and desolation, as God is constantly revealing himself to us in our experience.

In its simplest form, the Examen means asking ourselves questions to help us identify the 'consolations' and 'desolations' in our lives – 'the interior movements through which divine revelation unfolds.' We learn to recognise those things which give us life and energy or which drag energy away from us, leaving us feeling drained and empty instead of renewed and encouraged.

The Examen can also help us identify patterns in our responses which might need our attention, such as a tendency to avoid conflict or to keep silent instead of speaking out about something important. Consistent attention to these interior movements can help us resolve problems and discern a way forward which will enable us to live out our unique way of giving and receiving love. As we learn to use this tool for spiritual growth, we become more able to discern God's leading and to make life-giving decisions which enhance our humanity and our ministry.

The Examen is about asking ourselves two questions:

- For what am I most grateful?
- For what am I least grateful?

These questions can also be asked in other ways:

- When did I feel most alive today?
- When did I feel life draining out of me?
- What was today's high point?
- What was today's low point?
- What did I feel good about today?
- What was my biggest struggle today, or when did I feel sad, helpless or angry?

While daily practice is the ideal, in our busy lives it can be hard to maintain this discipline, but it is all the more important not to lose sight of where we can find God in our daily lives. It's an attitude more than a method.

EXAMEN PROCESS

Preparation:

You may wish to light a candle. Do whatever helps you to experience unconditional love. For example, imagine yourself in a favourite place with someone whose love you trust, such as a friend, Jesus or God, as you understand God.

Put your feet flat on the floor, take a few deep breaths from the bottom of your toes, up through your legs, your abdominal muscles and your chest. Breathe in that unconditional love, and when you breathe out, fill the space around you with it.

1. Place your hand on your heart and ask Jesus or God, as you understand God, to bring to your heart the moment today for which you are most grateful. If you could relive one moment, which one would it be? When were you most able to give and receive love today? Ask yourself what was said and done in that moment that made it so special. Breathe in the gratitude you felt and receive life again from that moment.

2. Ask God to bring to your heart the moment today for which you are least grateful. When were you least able to give and receive love? Ask yourself what was said and done in that moment that made it so difficult. Be with whatever you feel without trying to change or fix it in any way. You may wish to take deep breaths and let God's love fill you just as you are.

3. Give thanks for whatever you have experienced. If possible, share as much as you wish of these two moments with a friend.

❼ Appreciative feedback and simple evaluation activities

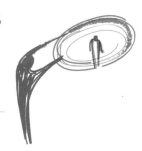

It is important to build into your AI practice simple and effective ways to evaluate the impact of what you have done.

Appreciative feedback

Appreciative feedback is a good way to gain an initial response to AI practice.

It provides constructive and reflective feedback that can enhance quality and support people engaging with new material. This can consist of two questions:

Activity

1. Ask people to feed back on each other's activities, such as drafting question protocols: 'What I most liked is …'
2. Then ask them to say: 'It could have been even better by …'

An example of appreciative feedback from the Methodist Church is given on page 61.

Valuation

This is a different take on evaluation. Typically, evaluation uses a tick list, comments on factors like the room, or quality of presentations and materials. This valuation identifies what people enjoyed, what they learned, and what actions individuals are going to take to support great conversations in the future.

Participants are asked to respond to each question on a Post-it note, numbering their answer according to the question. Everyone places their responses on a flip chart putting the numbered answer under the appropriately numbered question.

The feedback is then in public view. After the workshop, it's typed up and circulated to the participants.

Example questions:

Q1: What did you enjoy and find valuable in the workshop?

Q2: What did you learn from the process?

Q3: Name one thing you're going to do as a result of the workshop…

See page 54 for the completed valuation from the Christian Aid Forest Group workshop.

Helpful hints:

*   Practise appreciative feedback – it takes time and there's often an inbuilt tendency to criticise. Just think how you'd like to be treated.
*   Leave enough time to complete the valuation at the end of the workshop, and encourage people to read the comments before they leave;
*   Six months after the project design a conversation protocol with questions reflecting on the impact, achievements and learning;
*   Try including the appreciative feedback question 'what would make it even better?' into the valuation;
*   Encourage people to use their best handwriting, and remember to number the Post-it notes – it helps when you're writing them up.
*   Collect peoples' stories about the effects of using AI and create either a YouTube film or produce a mini book. One example is the hostel video on the Appreciating People web site: www.appreciatingpeople.co.uk.

Worship materials and liturgy to support the use of Appreciative Inquiry

PART FOUR

Worship materials and liturgy to support the use of Appreciative Inquiry

This section offers suggestions for worship materials and liturgies for introducing Appreciative Inquiry when the approach is being used with churches. You are invited to offer additional materials by sending them to the *Appreciating Church* website: www.appreciating.church.

We're very grateful for all the contributions to these worship resources. Material in the worship section has been provided by named authors, who are happy for their prayers and liturgies to be used in worship. If a prayer or other piece of work is printed for use in worship or other non-profit purposes, it should be credited to the named author and not altered. Permission must be sought in advance for any part of this publication to be reproduced in a commercial project, whether printed or digital. Please refer to the copyright information in the verso, on page ii.

Introduction

Worship itself is a supreme act of appreciation. Worship, through the Spirit, is generative. This doesn't mean that our worship of God always results in dramatic changes or actions. It may generate stillness or a sense of emptiness rather than filling-up.

This workbook already includes Bible references, quotes and real-life illustrations that can be used in acts of worship. Much of what you see in this section has been written by people who practice AI in their meetings and churches. Rather than AI being a tool or an add-on it is an integral part of their worshipping lives.

The following could be used to end or begin AI sessions or to introduce the whole idea of appreciation into services. Connections to the AI core principles are suggested in some cases.

Living in an appreciative way

Praise and Glory we present to you
for you are our lord.

All that we have comes from you.
Your whole creation is given to us as a gift.
Your love beams on us like the sun;
It burns into our very hearts,
And the light lives there,
to inspire, comfort and grow.

Great Father, we hold you in loving awe.

But there are times,
when things seem colder.
When the shadow of evil hides the sun
from our eyes,
blinded by our own inadequacies.

Then it is, that you show your loving mothers arms.
They enfold us, keep us warm,
comfort us, make us safe.

You are God for all
And you are God for each
You are God for us
And you are God for me.
Amen

Matthew Reed

Communion prayers

God of the table,
Host of hosts,
We keep returning here,
We keep coming back to bread and wine,
And we keep joining with Your people.
It's not that somehow this meal wears off,
It's not that our memories are that short,
Or that it's all too hard to understand,
(Although the more we come, the more we realise there is to understand)
It's just that we can't seem to live in the love that we see here.....
We thank and praise You for the love that gave birth to creation,
We thank and praise You for the love that nurtures and provides,
We thank and praise You for the love that rescued Your people from slavery and led them through the wilderness.
All of this seen in bread and wine and each other.
We thank and praise You for the love that chose to enter the human condition,
We thank and praise You for the love that sacrifices itself for others
We thank and praise You for the love that resists evil and death until newness comes
All of this seen in bread and wine and each other.
We thank and praise You for the love that brings joy,
We thank and praise You for the love that binds a community together,
And gives it courage to go beyond its walls to share good news,
All of this seen in bread and wine and each other.
We need to keep returning to this table, this bread and wine, this people.
They show us who we really are and who, by Your saving grace, we could be.
Host of hosts, thank you that there is a place for us here.
Amen.

Suzanne Nockels

We come to this table with glad thanksgiving –
God, you create the world we live in and you made us in your image:
creative and caring.
In scripture and history we learn of your continual attention and interest,
calling men and women in all times and places to challenge injustice and offer a better way.
We praise and thank you
that such love never ceases, even when your people have turned away.
In Jesus, we meet you in a life both like and unlike ours:
born into a loving family, yet called to show you to the world:
healing and teaching,
provoking and questioning,
laughing and crying.
And when the crowds rejected him and handed him over to trial and execution,
you gave him back to us.
Across time and space, we cannot but sing of your glory –
Holy, holy, holy Lord, God of power and might,
heaven and earth are full of your glory.
Hosanna in the highest.
Blessed is he who comes in the name of the Lord.
Hosanna in the highest.
Sending your Spirit to dance within and around us
to comfort and challenge,
we are strengthened and inspired to follow your call.
Be present now in this bread and wine
feeding us
filling us, body and blood,
to live in the world as the Body of Christ
loving and caring till the Kingdom comes.
Amen

Kathryn Price

No day but today

(adapt the examples to your own context)

This is our life now

The community worshipping on Sunday, regulars, visitors occasional and new, children and young people

Coming to meet God, listening for God's word, loving, admitting faults, receiving forgiveness, sharing concerns, sharing bread and wine

Pilots learning about the world they live in, having fun, playing games, making things

Women's fellowship meeting faithfully to pray, to talk to care for each other, to hear a visitor

The singers struggling with a new tune

A café for those who can't normally afford to eat out, stained glass workers, jujitsu classes, Cub Scouts, bands practicing

Our past life we rehearse and reprise often

Our future seems like a wish list

The coming year end and anniversary unintentionally encourage both

Just now, be still
Be still and know that I am God

There's only now – listen
There is never silence, there is a world living and breathing with us
God is in this world, in this place

There's only love
And love is to be enjoyed, savoured, given, known
Love is not always wishing things/people were as they used to be
Love is not always thinking about how much greener the grass is elsewhere
Love is not always wishing the time away in daydreams of an impossible tomorrow
Love takes time
Love looks
Love listens
Love feels
Love accepts

God, we say, is love
God, we say, is eternal
What does eternal mean if not here, now
Yes it means then and there also, but here and now is important for us
Here and now is where we are
Where love is concerned, eternal must mean no day but today
New every morning is the love . . .
At every moment God is striving for perfection, drawing us to the good, the best
And us?

We rush from here to there, making do, grabbing a bite, faster cars, longer hours, cramming more and more in
Reminiscing, regretting, planning, forecasting
Complaining of too little time

Take time
Take time to be with God, for God always has time for us
Time to be with God's people, for not all are able to rush any more and have too much time
Time to look at God's world and see its beauty and its destruction
Time to love and be loved

Jesus said: do not worry about tomorrow, it will have enough worries of its own

Jesus said: I will be with you always, to the end of the age

Hear the Word of God
Believe it, trust it, live it

Kathryn Price

St Bride's

Drawing on texts from the appreciative conversations and poems created during the process (see page 68 for the St Bride's AI story), these prayers were created for a service marking the 12-month anniversary of the start of the AI project. The worship theme was 'the wounded healer'.

The intention of St Bride's to be a safe sacred place for all emerged from the work. In the middle of the service, there were discussions in small groups on two questions: *What brought you to St Bride's? And what do you bring to St Bride's?* After the small group discussion there was an opportunity for people to share their experiences and stories.

Let us pray
God has no favourites
He bothered to give time and attention to the stranger
A refuge for the disillusioned
I'm not on my own,
Dead words broken open, give life to
To me
When I dare to be vulnerable
I'm not on my own
The flame of faith is kept alive
When I dare to be vulnerable
He bothered to give time and
attention to one stranger
God has no favourites

Let us pray
It gives us heart
A place of belonging, stillness and peace
It's how God created us
Community of the wounded
My deep call to serve others
Is how God created us
There's a feeling of walking into a sanctuary
My deep call to serve others
In the unplanned spaces that arise where God is

There's a feeling of walking into a sanctuary
Community of the wounded in the unplanned spaces that
Arise where God is
Give us heart
A place of belonging, stillness and peace

Releasing our fears

Let us pray

A presence

Opens doors for whoever wants to come in

Most of what he does is listen

Bring more heart centred

You totally accepted me

Most of what he does is listen
It felt like a shaft of light
You totally accepted me
Releasing people's gifts
It felt like a shaft of light
Being more heart centred
Releasing people's gifts
A presence
Opens doors for whoever wants to come in

Expressing Our Hopes

Let us pray

To forgive

I have discovered a language to express things
It calls me to lifestyle shifts
A new kind of freedom
Daring to dream dreams
To sit with doubts and mystery
It calls me to lifestyle shifts
A new kind of freedom
To sit with doubts and mystery
The divine enables me to move forward
A new kind of freedom
Daring to dream dreams
The divine enables me to move forward
I have found a language to express things to forgive

St Bride's

Simultaneity Principle

Finding love again: a creative liturgy

The kingdom of heaven is like treasure hidden in a field.

When a man found it he hid it again and then in his joy went and sold all he had and bought that field.

It might be good to project a picture of a field, or print an image for everyone
Why was the treasure in the field?
Why was something so precious and beautiful closed up and put out of sight where it risked never being found again?

I can imagine someone in the dark of night slipping out of the house and moving away the earth with his hands.

The dark times are good for burying parts of our humanity.

No-one will see. Tomorrow we will act just as we did before. Except a part of us will be missing – a certain sparkle that we have pushed deep down.

Why was the treasure in the field?
Was it because in some great chaos it was safer that way? It couldn't get knocked or stolen?
Was it because its shine reminded its owner of better times and now it was just too painful to look at?
Get rid of it, he told a servant and the servant did.
Was it meant to be buried for just a little while, for the duration of a crisis, but after a time did it just seem easier to leave it there?

I don't know why I question.
For you and I bury treasure all the time.
We bury our childish innocence,
our youthful enthusiasm.
We pile our cynicism and weariness upon them.
We bury our dreams,
those pictures we had of the people we might become,
people that made a difference in the world.
We pile sensibility over them,
say things like 'that was then – this is now'
or 'I'm too old for that kind of thing'.

We don't imagine that we could be as care-free as the children we once were, running down a slope on a windy day.
We don't imagine that we could experience the same thrill at being alive as standing on Waterloo Bridge and seeing the capital stretch out before us, thinking 'I'm part of this great city'.
We don't imagine that we could have the same sense of belonging as we did in our lover's arms.
Or the same sense of inner peace as when the sun sets over the fells.
It is impossible to go back, it's gone; buried back in time.

We bury hope by calling it naivety or 'not being realistic'.
We box up faith and say we're too wise for that now.
Worst of all, we bury love or we bury the potential to love.
We can't love a fellow human being because we bitter.
We can't love a fellow human being because we cannot forgive.
Love is either too hard or it has no place in our lives anymore.
Pieces of heaven that we no longer want to look at.

It's true we can't go back again.
But our 'never say never' God will not let the treasure of the kingdom stay submerged forever.
He looks at the well-worked field of our lives and says 'again' –
again you will laugh
again you will dream
again you will hope
again your faith will rise
again love will stir within you
again.

And so a new face, a new person, a new circumstance comes and gently brushes away our earth and in some corner of our heart-land a quiet resurrection happens and our treasure once more sees the light.

Hand round scraper boards

I love restoration programmes on the television. Somehow it always seems glorious to me when a hidden garden layout is revealed from something that just looks like a rubbish dump, or someone gets out a hanky and rubs on a painting and all the true colours come through.

You have been handed what looks like a grubby piece of card. You might be able to detect colour underneath but it has been buried.

It strikes me that Jesus was in the restoration or recovery business. He stood in the synagogue and declared that he would liberate the captives, recover the sight of the blind, and free the oppressed. He would move away with his life the poverty, the persecution, the sadness, the sin that buried the brightness of human beings. In a short while I'd like you to think of what you would ask Jesus to recover in you – what has been buried that you would like to come to the surface again?

And I ask you to scratch that word into the black wax – like this *(demonstrate)*. When you've done that – when you've made your prayer, you can come and place it around the cross and perhaps read what others have written and pray for them.

It's just one word so no one will know your precise situation. If you don't want to write, you could draw a picture or a symbol.

Play some music and end with a prayer of blessing.

Suzanne Nockels

Letting go of stones

(The woman caught in adultery – John 8.1-11)

I was so angry. I have never been so angry. I have never been swept up in so much anger. How dare she! How dare she go against what was right! How dare she spit on all that I hold dear. How dare she unsettle our whole community! How many people has she hurt? She will bring the wrath of God down upon our heads.

They dragged her from the house, the teachers must have been watching, and they took her through the streets to the wandering preacher from Nazareth. She looked a mess. She looked like the fallen woman she was. They asked the preacher what he thought. Should she be stoned? The woman howled and begged for mercy. They piled up the evidence. They quoted from the Law of Moses. Which side was he on? Was he righteous or did he condone her behaviour? After all he was friends with publicans and tax-collectors. Question after question – flying like stones. There was no way out of this. It was clear that there was only one option. Not to participate was to become as bad as her. I searched the ground and found a suitable stone.

The preacher said . . . nothing . . . He simply doodled in the sand. We all looked and tried to see something in the patterns or the shapes. What was he doing? It's only now that I realise what he was up to. He was taking the attention away from her; letting the heat of our anger dissipate in the stillness.

He slowly straightened up and said 'Let any one of you who is without sin be the first to cast the stone'. It was as if we had simply interrupted his day-dreaming, because he went back to doodling in the sand.

We looked at each other. Who was going to go first then? I couldn't. My sin loomed large in my memory. Last year I could see that our small crop was about to be ruined by the weather – so, unseen, I had harvested what I could – on the Sabbath. Every sweep of the scythe had cut my soul.

I could hear the thud, thud, as people let go of their stones and walked away; the eldest first – maybe because maturity brought a certain honesty. I wanted to stay angry. I wanted to stay superior and use her as a way of making myself feel better, but I couldn't. One by one my fingers released the stone. As it fell I felt a burden, a guilt drop from my soul.

There is always another way. There is always a different question, a different place to start. We can start with stones and moral cul-de-sacs or we can let the silence speak.

Suzanne Nockels

Anticipatory Principle

Walking on the water

Lord the life of this world is like the rough choppy waters of the open sea
and yet you call us to walk on the waves
so we pray
for all who are damaged by the storms of life: living with violence, abuse, exploitation, neglect
Give them grace and courage **to walk on the waves**
for all who are wearied by the struggle: dealing with loss – of health, of loved ones, of work and home, of self-esteem
Give them grace and courage **to walk on the waves**
for all who feel excluded and will not accept that the call is to them too
Give them grace and courage **to walk on the waves**

And if the world is that rough sea, then our communities must offer the safety of the boat
so we pray
when we see a hand held out for support
Give us grace and love to **welcome and restore**
when we recognise fellow rescuers who are not part of our group
Give us grace and love to **welcome and restore**
when we must risk all for the sake of another
Give us grace and love to **welcome and restore**

Lord, hear our prayer

In the name of Jesus who calls us out and in the power of the Spirit who lifts us up
Amen

Kathryn Price

Poetic Principle

Flower, Hand, Heart liturgy

Distribute flowers, one for each person present.
Look at this flower.
Such deep colours,
Intricate patterns,
What detail!
Balanced to perfection.
Loved in its making.

Silence to appreciate God's Creation

We thank you Lord
For all that you give us.
We marvel at your beautiful imagination
Awestruck by your power,
So softly and luxuriously expressed.

You hold this flower in your hand
And what a hand
So wonderfully constructed,
Fantastic mechanisms – And it lives!
All it can do, all it has done,
Maybe not as strong or as sure as it has been,
But think of all that it has held,
All it has stroked,
All it has operated
And it is just a hand.
And your neighbour has one too.

Silence to appreciate all that God gives us

We thank you Lord
For all that you give us.
We marvel at your beautiful imagination
Awestruck by your power,
So softly and luxuriously expressed.
You look at your heart,
And at your life.
Glorious moments of joy and fun,
Times of sadness and pain,
of regret and sorrow
Periods of deep uncertainty
But others of confidence, clarity or security.
All a pattern of the Spirit
As we serve the Lord,
Knowing and unknowing

Silence to appreciate God's love for us as people.

We thank you Lord
For all that you give us.
We marvel at your beautiful imagination
Awestruck by your power,
So softly and luxuriously expressed.
You look at the flower,
You glimpse the father, the creator God,
You look at your hand, you glimpse Jesus, for these are his hands, commissioned for his work.
You look at your heart, you glimpse the Spirit, God's empowering love active in you.
We thank you Lord
For all that you give us.
We marvel at your beautiful imagination
Awestruck by your power,
So softly and luxuriously expressed.
Amen

Matthew Reed

Perfume

Read John 12: 1-8
Did the perfume linger Lord?
In the days ahead did you catch its fragrance?
Like honeysuckle on the breeze.
Did it take to you back to the beautiful thing;
The evening spent with friends,
The last time you were touched with gentleness?

When the holy turned to hate
Did it remind you of the temple?
Against the metallic smell of your own blood
Did it provide a note of care?
When bones were broken
Did you smell crushed roses?
In the reeking stench of death
Was there still an undertone of love?
I hope so.

What lingers
What remains
What stays
May be as insubstantial as perfume in the wind.
But it is more solid than anything.

Suzanne Nockels

Consider the lilies

'Consider how the wild flowers grow. They do not labour or spin. Yet I tell you, not even Solomon in all his splendour was dressed like one of these'

The word 'consider' in New Testament Greek means not a quick glance but 'to deeply learn from'. Observing or watching implies a passive act and looking should be active and engaged. However, looking can also sound like an imperative 'hey- you must look at this'. Take time, slow down, don't force meaning, soak up what you are seeing and return to it again and again.

Show a copy of Stanley Spencer's painting 'Christ in the Wilderness- Consider the Lillies'. You can find it here: http://www.wikiart.org/en/stanley-spencer/christ-in-the-wilderness-consider-the-lilies. Ask people to spend time focused on the picture. Ask them just to take in the colours, the detail, the size and position of things. Allow at least three minutes of quiet contemplation.

Then as a group discuss the following. Remember this is an artwork – there are no wrong or right interpretations, just the association that individuals make.

- Despite 'lilies' being in the title of the painting why do you think Stanley Spencer has painted different flowers?
- What does the position of the Christ figure remind you of?
- What do you make of the difference in size between Christ and the daisies?
- It is almost as if Christ and the wild flowers are looking and talking to each other. What do you think they might be saying?
- When was the last time you 'stayed with' an artwork or something in the natural world and it taught you something valuable?
- This is part of a series called 'Christ in the Wilderness'. Does this painting fit/not fit with experiences of spiritual wilderness?
- After looking at, and discussing this painting how might considering the flowers either relieve anxiety or undermine our trust in status and riches?.

Then come back to the painting and look at it together again before reading the prayer below.

Jesus who looked first and looked long,
Help us not dismiss the unspectacular,
Help us stay with those things which will not give up their secrets easily,

Help us find beauty in surprisingly simple places,
Like a dandelion poking through cracked concrete.
We thank you for the sights that have fed our souls
The ones we return to in our gallery of memories.
Considering Christ, help us learn deeply
For these precious, unpurchaseable things show us how to live free in this world.
Amen.

Suzanne Nockels

Visions and dreams

Arthur Stace grew up in Sydney, Australia. He was a child of alcoholics who searched bins for scraps of food. At 15, he too hit the bottle as a way to escape. He was sent to jail, came out and worked as a scout for his sister's brothel. In 1916 he enlisted in the army and saw action in World War One. He heard two great sermons which captured his imagination and he gave his heart to Jesus. Revd John Ridley's sermon included these words – 'Eternity, Eternity, I wish that I could sound or shout that word to everyone in Sydney. You've got to meet it. Where will you spend Eternity?' Stace later said, 'Eternity went ringing through my brain and suddenly I began crying and felt a powerful call from the Lord to write Eternity'. This was a man who was illiterate and could hardly write his own name, yet when he wrote 'Eternity', he did so in a beautiful copperplate style.

For the next 35 years he wrote it all over the city, getting up at 5am so as not to be spotted. He wrote it some 500,000 times. The 'eternity man' became the stuff of urban legend. In 1963 a photographer spotted him coming out of the church where he worked as a cleaner. Stace stopped and wrote on the pavement. He took two pictures before Stace disappeared. Two of his inscriptions are in the National Museum of Australia, where they have inspired a whole gallery. Another is inside the bell of the General Post Office Tower, though no-one knows how it got there. At the 2000 Olympics, his 'Eternity' was lit up on Sydney Harbour Bridge.

Positive Principle

Dare to dream

To the tune 'Woodlands' ('Tell out, my soul')

We're not alone! God speaks and helps us know:
God sees all people's pain and hears their cries.
Through burning bush, God tells us we should go,
like Moses, go and help the slaves arise!

But who are we to hope we might be heard,
and dare to dream that slavery still could end?
We're not alone! So do not be deterred:
God says, 'I will be with you as your friend.'

We're not alone! God's Spirit gives us power
to bring good news to those in poverty.
Through prophecy, God says this very hour
like Jesus we've the word of liberty!

But who are we to think we understand
and dare to dream the system could be fair?
We're not alone! God's Spirit is at hand
to help us help each other truly share.

We're not alone! The Spirit's dancing flames
transform us so we strive as dreamers must.
Through burning bush and prophet God proclaims
we're called to make a world that is more just!

Graham Adams

Graham is a congregational minister and theological educator who has been working in inner-city Openshaw, East Manchester, since 2002.

Feeding the five thousand

'You give them something to eat.'

What kind of answer is that? It's up there with 'Let them eat cake!' Jesus have you seen the size of this crowd? How much money do you think we've got? Do you think we've been stashing it away while we've been wandering about the countryside with you? Do you think that some of us are getting banker's bonuses without you knowing? We don't have the resources. We don't have the money. We don't have the time (Jesus, it's late). We don't have the energy of people (there's only twelve of us).

We have a crowd of needs in our area but we don't have the right building, the support, the money to pay for a community worker – our minister is on quarter-time.

We have a crowd of opportunities in our area but we don't have the technology, the publicity, the youngsters with get-up-and-go. We don't have guitars.

We can't feed these people.

Jesus looks at us and asked' How many loaves do you have'. 'Go and see'. Go and honestly see not what you haven't got, but what you have. Sit down, gather in expectation, form new relationships.

Even if it's the equivalent of five loaves and two fish. Place them in His hands, pray and let the sharing begin.

Suzanne Nockels

115

God has no favourites

He bothered to give time and attention to one stranger
a refuge for the disillusioned.
The flame of faith is kept alive
and dead words broken open, give life to me,

a refuge for the disillusioned.
I'm not on my own,
dead words broken open, give life to me
when I dare to be vulnerable.

I'm not on my own.
The flame of faith is kept alive
when I dare to be vulnerable.
He bothered to give time and attention to one stranger,
God has no favourites.

St Bride's

Opening prayers

We rise to the dawning of life;
Countless beings sing the hymn of creation.
We feel the spirit moving in all things;
The earth, sky and sea bring us healing.
We touch the humming lines of connection;
The web of all things sparkles with energy.

May the Spirit of creation, healing and connection
Bless and hold this space, this time, this being-together.
And may all that we bring and all that we are
Find a welcome in the silence.

Silence

Through the spaces of our city,
Public and private,
Sacred and profane,
Neglected and contested,
Divided and united,
Commercial and communal,
The Spirit makes its exile way:
Seeking a home,
Seeking a face,
Seeking a listening ear.
Spirit of God,
Be with us here.

Through the spaces of our lives
Confused and radiant,
Hurting and healing,
Anxious and confident,
Ashamed and proud,
Beautiful and broken,
The Spirit walks the inner path:
Seeking the truth,
Seeking the soul,
Seeking the child within.
Spirit of God
Be with us here.

Steven Shakespeare, St Bride's

Invitation to communion

All are welcome in this place.

With our conflicts and fears,
Human in our vulnerability.
All are welcome in this place
With our doubts and questions,
Longing for a living truth.
All are welcome in this place
With our queerness and unspoken dreams,
Seeking a space to be ourselves.
All are welcome in this place
With our gifts, celebrated and unsung,
Trusting that here we are known.
All are welcome in this place

With all who need food and drink and companionship;
With all who are simply human;
With all living things;
We are welcome in this place.

In silence, we pause to remember that we are welcome,
And to bring to mind those who are not physically present,
But who are with us in spirit.

Jesus said that many would come from east and west to eat at the table of the kingdom.

He ate with those who were called sinners and unclean without asking them to make themselves pure or 'normal'.

He was the guest at many tables.

And finally, he was the host, when he shared his life, his living companionship, with those he called friends.

**May this be a table of meeting, of inclusion, of liberation, from all that breeds hatred, prejudice and division.
In the name of Jesus. Amen.**

Steven Shakespeare, St Bride's

A small selection of other resources:

Hymns:

Dare to dream, Fred Kaan from his book The Only Earth We Know © 1999 Stainer & Bell / Hope Publishing Company

I dream of a church, Kate Compston Words © 1994 Hope Publishing Company

Songs to shake us up 200 new hymn texts with well known tunes to challenge church and society. John Campbell. © 2016 Kevin Mayhew Publishers.

Prayers and other worship material:

* *A wee worship book: 4th edition;* Wild Goose Worship Group (have a look at their other material too)
* *Making liturgy: creating rituals for worship and life*, edited by Dorothea McEwan, Pat Pinsent, Ianthe Pratt, Veronica Seddon © 2001 Canterbury Press
* *Psalms Redux, Poems and Prayers* Carla Grosch Miller © 2014 Canterbury Press
* *Meditation on a Hazelnut,* from Revelations of Divine Love, Julian of Norwich

Online resources:

* The Peace Pole project http://www.peacepoleproject.org/index.html
* Prayer of Examen http://www.ignatianspirituality.com/ignatian-prayer/the-examen
* Steven Shakespeare, Prayers for an Inclusive Church (Canterbury Press, 2008).

Thanks to Suzanne Nockels, Congregational Federation and Katheryn Price, URC, for developing and co-ordinating this worship resource and many other people who made contributions. Additional worship materials will included on the *Appreciating Church* website.

The story of Appreciating Church, its development, and how to get involved

PART FIVE

The story of Appreciating Church, its development, and how to get involved

This is the story of how *Appreciating Church* developed, and its outline plans for further development.

UK church interest in AI has deep and varied roots, going back to the late 1990s. An introductory guide to AI by the Church of Scotland from 2009 is available online (see reading list on page 123). One strand of the United Reformed Church's interest in AI dates from 2004 through Revd Roberta Rominger, the then Moderator of Thames North Synod. The seed planted grew into a denominational conference in 2009 led by Mark Lau Branson, author of *Memories, Hopes and Conversations*, which is also included in *Appreciating Church's* reading list. There have been similar AI developments in other denominations.

Appreciating Church's gestation period began in 2013 with a series of informal conversations initiated by Revd Jane Weedon of Welwyn Garden City URC, which resulted in an *AI Essentials* course, facilitated by Appreciating People in March 2014 at the URC's Windermere Centre. Participants were drawn from the URC and the Congregational Federation. The Methodist Church expressed interest in what was being done a few months later, as did people involved in Appreciating People's work with both Quakers and a Church of England parish in Liverpool.

After a period of testing and reflection, a delivery model was developed which offers tailored local introductory AI training provision based on *Taste of AI*[1]. Additional advanced AI training at a regional or national level, to both deepen AI practice and create a pool of local AI trainers, was also developed. The first of these *Developing Your AI* Practice events took place at the Windermere Centre in February 2016 with a further course in November 2016.

From the outset, the strategy has been to create a self-sustaining community of AI practice, embedded in the partner denominations, and backed up by appropriate training resources. To support long term sustainability, a training pathway has been created with Appreciating People, which enables AI practitioners to progress through apprenticing, co-facilitating and leading AI training programmes. Appreciating People's role in the project is to advise, coach, train in AI, and provide quality assurance.

Part of the process to co-design and co-create the *Appreciating Church* resource included bringing together an ecumenical group to discuss and provide biblical reference and church examples for inclusion in the publication, introducing their insights and experience.

News of latest developments and a timeline on the use of AI within the partner churches can be found on: www.appreciating.church.

The AI community of practice includes both practitioners and practitioner-trainers. News of opportunities to deepen practice can be found on the website: www.appreciating.church.

The *Appreciating Church* accreditation pathway for aspiring AI trainers and facilitators is:

- Participation in a *Taste of AI* workshop or AI basics course;
- A period of AI practice and journaling;
- Participation in the three day residential *Developing Your AI Practice*;
- Apprenticing delivery of the *Taste of AI course*, mentored by an existing facilitator accredited by Appreciating People;
- Taking the lead on delivery of the *Taste of AI* course with Appreciating People coaching support.

The *Appreciating Church* website: www.appreciating.church, carries information about existing AI training opportunities, as well as contacts for supplying a certified AI trainer/facilitator to deliver a local and bespoke Taste of AI course.

---

1   *Taste of AI* 2.0 is an Appreciative Inquiry resource pack created by Appreciating People

Acknowledgements, further reading and information on Appreciating People

PART SIX
Acknowledgements, further reading and information on Appreciating People

Further reading

These publications have particularly influenced the development of the thinking and ideas for *Appreciating Church.*

Appreciative Inquiry: change at the speed of imagination (Second edition)
Jane Magruder Watkins, Bernard Mohr, and Ralph Kelly
Pfeiffer: (2011)

Appreciative Living: the principles of Appreciative Inquiry in personal life
Jackie Kelm: Venet (2005)

Now discover your strengths
Marcus Buckingham and Donald O. Clifton: The Free Press (2006)

Authentic Happiness
Martin E.P. Seligman Atria Paperback (2002) and website on positive psychology from University of Pensylvania https://www.authentichappiness.sas.upenn.edu/

VIA survey of character strengths
Research shows that character strengths can be used to address a variety of life challenges and achieve positive personal and community outcomes.

Have a look at www.viacharacter.org/www/

AI essentials – a practical, straightforward and easy to use guide to Appreciative Inquiry
Wordscapes (2013)

Food for Thought: a journal for appreciating daily life
Wordscapes (2012)

United Religions Initiative
URI is a global grassroots interfaith network that cultivates peace and justice by engaging people to bridge religious and cultural differences and work together for the good of their communities and the world. www.uri.org/about_uri/charter and www.uri.org/cooperation_circles/create_a_cooperation_circle

AI Practitioner is a quarterly journal and digital resource. Find the website here: www.aipractitioner.com

Spirituality and Appreciative Inquiry

aipractitioner.com/product/appreciative-inquiry-practitioner-november-2014/

Appreciative Inquiry for Collaborative Solutions: 21 Strength-Based Workshops
Robyn Stratton-Berkessel
Pfeiffer (John Wiley & Sons), 2010

Positive psychology at work: how positive leadership and Appreciative Inquiry create inspiring organisations
Sarah Lewis: Wiley Blackwell (2011)

Positive Psychology and Change How leadership, collaboration and Appreciative Inquiry create Transformational results
Sarah Lewis: Wiley Blackwell (2016)

POSITIVITY : Groundbreaking Research Reveals How to Embrace the Hidden Strength of Positive Emotions, Overcome Negativity, and Thrive
Barbara L. Fredrickson, (2009)

Claiming the Light: Appreciative Inquiry and Congregational Transformation
Paul C. Chaffee
Chapter 4 in *www. congregationalresources.org – a guide to congregational resources for building congregational vitality*, Richard Bass, Editor (Alban Institute, 2005)

Appreciative Inquiry: An introductory guide for use in the Church of Scotland
Sheena Orr, December 2009
http://www.churchofscotland.org.uk/__data/assets/pdf_file/0013/20434/appreciative_inquiry_introductory_guide.pdf

Creating Great Conversations
Tim Slack: Wordscapes (2013)

How to Be More Awesome: An appreciative journal (for young people aged 14 to 25)
Tim Slack and Suzanne Quinney: Wordscapes (2014)

How to Be More Awesome – Student Planner Edition (for young people aged 14 to 25)
Tim Slack and Suzanne Quinney: Wordscapes (2016)

Zen and the art of Appreciative Inquiry
Roger Rowett: Roger Rowett (2012)

Appreciative Inquiry in Higher Education – a transformative force
Jeanie Cockell and Joan McArthur-Blair: Jossey-Bass (2012)

Appreciative Leadership
Diana Whitney, Amanda Trosten Bloom, Kae Rader: McGraw and Hill (2010)

Appreciative Leaders – in the Eye of the Beholder
Marjorie Schiller, Bea Mah Holland and Deanna Riley; Taos Institute

Memories, Hopes and Conversations: Appreciative Inquiry and congregational change (2nd edition).
Mark Lau Branson: Rowman and Littlefield (2014)

Sharing God's Blessing – how to renew the local church
Roger Greenwood: SPCK (2016)

Turn the Ship Around! A True Story of turning followers into leaders – Building Leaders by Breaking the Rules
David Marquet (2013)

Thanks

Thanks to all the people who have contributed AI experiences, shared AI practice and generally encouraged and been generative in all their actions. New friendships and relationships have been formed. There have been contributors to the AI experiences and stories, providers of worship materials and project supporters. Thanks to participants in the task and finish group and the workshop on Bible and spirituality at Luther King House in March 2016. Thanks to the United Reformed Church for allocating staff time and resources, the URC legacy fund, and the Methodist Church for part-funding development of this resource.

A particular thanks goes to Jane Weedon, URC minister in Welwyn Garden City. Jane introduced Appreciating People to Fiona Thomas, URC. Without that introduction and original vision, *Appreciating Church* would not have happened. Thanks also to Roberta Rominger who set this all off by giving Mark Lau Branson's book to Jane and introducing Fiona to AI back in 2004.

Thank you to our contributors and supporters

Richard Andrews, Richard Armiger, Kieran Bohan, Helen Bush, Jim Coleman, Jack Dyce, Guy Elsmore, Lindsey Godwin, Elizabeth Gray King, Zélie Gross, Julie Hanna, David Hanson, Ralph Kelly, Holly Langley, Mark Lau Branson, Philippa Linton, Jane Magruder Watkins, Sian McArthur, Suzanne Nockels, Lynne Norman, Kathryn Price, Matthew Reed, Roberta Rominger, Steven Shakespeare, Oliver Waterhouse, Kevin Watson and Jane Weedon.

Enormous thanks to members of the 'task and finish' group, who provided much guidance and support in the creation of this publication. See the inside back cover for further information.

Particular thanks goes to Suzanne Quinney for her support and guidance in providing AI experience and editing skills, and to Fiona Shaw for her patience in the editing and production process.

Acknowledgements

Appreciating People works with people, communities, business, charities and organisations to help them get the best out of themselves. Working regionally, nationally and internationally from its base in Liverpool, UK, Appreciative Inquiry lies at the heart of everything it does. Its work supports organisational development, resilience, adaptability, innovation and wellbeing across local authorities, private businesses, communities, hospitals, universities and social enterprises.

Appreciating People is the principle AI training provider and coach for the *Appreciating Church* programme and partners with the David L Cooperidder at the Center for AI Champlain College in Vermont, USA.

AI essentials is a range of products and resources written by Appreciating People and published by Wordscapes. Appreciating People also provides short courses in the practical application of AI. For more information about the company and its products see www.appreciatingpeople.co.uk.

Illustrator: Elizabeth Gray-King
A classically trained professional artist, Elizabeth Gray-King is a visual theologian and an ordained minister in the United Reformed Church, working as its Education and Learning Programme Officer. With a studio on the Grand Union Canal, she illustrates books and journals, exhibits paintings widely, creates worship installations and is frequently Artist in Residence at conferences to create visual theological reflections.
www.elizabethgrayking.com

Kieran Bohan – *Appreciating Church* website designer
Kieran's varied career mixes pastoral and creative roles. Originally a teacher, he began training as a Catholic priest, then left to work with vulnerable adults and retrain in media and marketing. He now works part time as chaplain to Liverpool YMCA and as Communications Officer for Modern Church, an international society promoting liberal Christian theology. He was a founder member of the Open Table worship community for LGBT Christians in 2008, and was commissioned in March 2016 as a Local Missional Leader by the Archdeacon of Liverpool to support LGBT Christians through spiritual practice, pastoral care, education and advocacy.

Wordscapes
Wordscapes is an award-winning non-fiction publisher and storyteller. Based in Liverpool, Wordscapes works with clients locally, nationally and internationally, publishing a range of both traditional hardback and paperbacks alongside a number of eBooks. Fields include local interest, business (marketing, HR and leadership), cookery and celebratory anniversary/ occasion titles.

Wordscapes also works on a range of communication projects for clients, developing organisational storytelling to create an authentic, memorable narratives. For more information, have a look at www.wordscape.org.uk.

Notes

Notes

Notes